THE SPIRAL OF TIME SERIES

RAV DOVBER PINSON

THE MONTH of IYYAR

vol **2**

◆• EVOLVING THE SELF | LAG B'OMER •◆

IYYUN PUBLISHING

THE MONTH OF IYYAR © 2018 DovBer Pinson. All rights reserved. No part of this book may be used or reproduced in any manner whatsoever without written permission except in the case of brief quotations embodied in critical articles and reviews.

    Published by IYYUN Publishing
    232 Bergen Street
    Brooklyn, NY 11217

http://www.iyyun.com

Iyyun Publishing books may be purchased for educational, business or sales promotional use. For information please contact: contact@IYYUN.com

Editor: Reb Matisyahu Brown

Developmental Editor: Reb Eden Pearlstein

Proofreading: Alyssa Elbogen

Proofreading / Editing: Simcha Finkelstein

Cover and book design: RP Design and Development

Cover image: Illustration by Adar Darnov
© 2015 Deuteronomy Press, used with publisher's permission as a gift to the Iyyun Center.
See **www.circlecalendar.com** *for more information.*

pb ISBN: 978-0-9914720-7-9

Pinson, DovBer 1971-
The Month of Iyyar: Evolving the Self and Lag B'Omer
1.Judaism 2. Jewish Spirituality 3. General Spirituality

vol **2**

THE MONTH *of* IYYAR

EVOLVING THE SELF | LAG B'OMER

IYYUN PUBLISHING

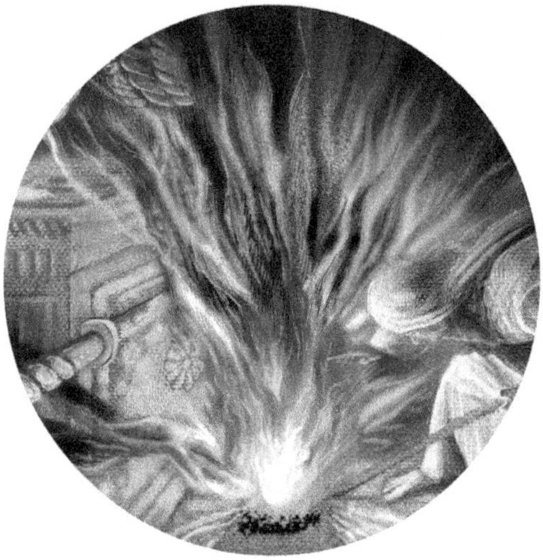

DEDICATED

TO

THE FRIEDMAN
BARR
MARKOWITZ
AND
BERKIN FAMILY
שיחי'

וזכות התורה הק' וסיועם
תעמוד להם לנחת מכל צאצאיהם
ואך טוב וחסד ירדפום כל ימי חייהם אמן ואמן

*May the month of Healing
and the Zechus / merit of
Rabbi Shimon bar Yochai
bring healing and perfect health,
boundless Nachas,
and an abundance of
Material and Spiritual Prosperity
to the entire family.*

CONTENTS

3 | OPENING

Part One:
THE MONTH OF IYYAR

5 | **Between Self-Expression and Soul-Development**

9 | *Permutation of Hashem's Name*

11 | *Torah Verse*

14 | *Letter*

17 | *Name of the Month*

26 | *Sense*

29 | *Sign*

32 | *Tribe*

36 | *Body Part*

39 | *Element*

41 | *Torah Portions*

43 | *Season of the Year*

Part Two:
LAG B'OMER

| 65 | CHAPTER ONE
       **An In-Depth Expoloration Into the Roots
       and Significance of this Special Day**

| 141 | CHAPTER TWO
       Customs & Practices of Lag B'Omer
       • *Bonfires* • *Meron: Grave of Rashbi* • *Bows & Arrows*
       • *Parades* • *Upsherin* • *Zohar, Songs in Honor of Rashbi*

| 165 | CHAPTER THREE
       Essays on the Omer & Lag B'Omer

| 166 | *Creating Balance through Counting the Omer*

| 174 | *Hod shebe'Hod / Splendor of Splendor*

| 177 | *Longing to See the Face of Elokim*

| 185 | *Unifying Separation*

OPENING

Each month of the year radiates with a distinct quality, providing unique opportunities for personal growth and illumination. Accordingly, every month has a slightly different climate and represents a particular stage in the "story of the year" as expressed through the annual cycles of nature. The winter months call for practices and pursuits that are intrinsically different than those of the summer months. Some months are filled with holidays, some have only one, still others are left without. Each month therefore has its own natural and spiritual signature.

According to the deeper levels of Torah, each month's distinct qualities, opportunities, and natural phenomena correspond to a 12-part symbolic structure. The spiritual nature of each month is thus articulated according to its unique entries for each of these 12 points of light, which include: 1) a permutation of Hashem's Four-Letter name, 2) a verse from the Torah, 3) a letter of the

Aleph Beis, 4) the name of the month itself, 5) an experiential "sense," 6) a Zodiac sign, 7) a tribe of Israel, 8) a body part, 9) an element, 10) a unit of successive Torah portions that are read during the month, 11) a season of the year, and 12) the holidays that occur during the month.

By reflecting on these twelve themes, an ever-ascending spiral of insight, understanding, and practical action, becomes revealed. Learning to navigate and harness the nature of change, by holistically engaging with the cycles of time, adds a deeper sense of purpose and heightened presence to our lives.

In this present volume we will delve into the spiritual nature of the month of Iyyar according to these twelve categories.

NOTE: *For a more comprehensive treatment of this 12-part system and the overarching dynamics of the "story of the year," an in-depth introduction has been provided in Volume One of this series, The Spiral of Time: Unraveling the Yearly Cycle.*

PART ONE:

THE MONTH OF IYYAR
BETWEEN SELF-EXPRESSION AND SOUL DEVELOPMENT

Iyyar marks the beginning of the second month of spring. In the previous month of Nisan, we officially moved out of our winter hibernation, so to speak. This seasonal and spiritual transition is celebrated on *Pesach* / Passover and is symbolized by the Exodus from Egypt. Following this miraculous birth into freedom and vitality, we now begin to feel more self-assured and expressive in Iyyar. Due to the warming weather, we are more relaxed and comfortable being outside. Freedom is in the air, not just as a budding potential, but as a blossoming reality. We are naturally pulled in numerous exciting directions, whether towards new adventures, opportunities, or relationships. And this is precisely where the inner work of this month comes into play.

After the initial excitement of spring sets in, and we have literally and figuratively opened our doors and gone outside, we may start to feel a bit over-exposed and vulnerable. One possible response to this feeling of vulnerability may lead us to believe that others around us are a threat, and we can thus become more assertive, loud, or even aggressive. On the other hand, vulnerability can also bring up an opposite reaction, leading us to retreat further into ourselves. Both of these psycho-emotional reactions — excessive assertiveness and excessive introspection — are deeply related to the precise mental, emotional, and spiritual work that needs to be done during the month of Iyyar.

Nisan, the first month of spring, marks a time of accentuated gratitude; spring is here and new possibilities are opening for us. In Iyyar, spring is already a given fact. We may therefore take our newfound feelings of vitality, expansiveness, and expressiveness for granted. When something is new, we are often more cautious and respectful of its power. Once we feel we have settled into something, we may not be as careful as we once were. A false sense of mastery may set in, blinding us to the potholes and pitfalls that still remain in our path. Therefore, during this time of year we must work to balance our newly emergent energy and excitement with a conscious commitment to self-refinement and right-relationship. This is achieved through a daily practice known as *Sefiras haOmer* / Counting the Omer; which, as we will learn, is ultimately intended to be an initiation into the deeper rhythms of time as well as an active and gradual rectification of our *Midos* / interpersonal attributes.

Nisan, the first month in the cycle of months, is associated with

Avraham / Abraham, and the attribute of *Chesed* / kindness and openness. Iyyar is connected with *Yitzchak* / Isaac, and the attribute of *Gevurah* / strength and restriction. The subsequent month, Sivan, is associated with *Ya'akov* / Jacob and the attribute of *Tiferes* / balanced compassion.

After our spiritual birth, as it were, during the Exodus from Egypt (commemorated during *Pesach*) followed by our infancy in the latter part of Nisan, comes the month of Iyyar in which we begin to grow up and start to express our individuality. Iyyar thus represents our childhood and adolescence, following the birth and infancy of Nisan.

Our sages draw a parallel between an infant and the sign of the *Taleh* / Aries / lamb (the zodiac sign of Nisan). A tender and meek infant grows a little older and becomes stronger like a *Shor* / Taurus / young bull (the sign of Iyyar) (*Tanchuma*, Ha'azinu). The child - and later adolescent - begins to strongly express their individuality, but this assertiveness can turn, if not checked, into a kind of arrogance and aggression. Therefore we need to ensure that our new assertiveness, coming from out of 'winter dormancy,' does not manifest at the expense of others. We *do* need to affirm ourselves and become individuals; in a way that is healthy and respectful of ourselves as well as others.

As mentioned, Iyyar is a month of *Gevurah* / strength and power, but not only for outward movement and manifestation; this *Gevurah* can also give us strength for inwardness, introspection, and self-evaluation. When we go through Iyyar with proper *Kavanah* / intention and awareness, we will then mature into adulthood as well-adjusted, emotionally stable, and mindful individuals, ready to receive the Torah during the next month of Sivan. This is the overarching theme of Iyyar. Now let us explore the details.

PERMUTATION OF HASHEM'S NAME

There are four letters in the Name of Hashem (Yud-Hei-Vav-Hei) and each month of the year has an inner light that 'shines' through a different permutation of these four letters. Each permutation communicates a different spiritual dynamic encoded within the Divine signature of the particular month. In the month of Iyyar, the letter sequence of Hashem's name is Yud-Hei-Hei-Vav (The vowels in the sequence are Yud-Chirik, Hei-Patach, Hei-Patach, and Vav-Sh'va). This particular permutation includes two letters in their normal sequence, Yud-Hei, and two letters in reverse sequence, Hei-Vav (instead of Vav-Hei). In general, an inverse sequence of letters indicates the presence of *Din* / judgment, severity, or separation, whereas the letters arranged in their intended sequence indicates a flow of *Chesed* / kindness, love, and unity (*Zohar* 2, 186a.; see also, "Backwards is the secret of Gevurah," *Zohar* 2, 52a). Iyyar offers us an experience of these two opposite energy flows in combination. The month embodies a quality of *Din*, a sense of separation and thus longing, as well as a sense of *Chesed*, deep unity and connection.

TORAH VERSE

Each month is associated with a particular Torah verse, which is connected to the month's permutation of the Divine Name. The order of the letters in the Divine Name for each month provides an acronym for each month's particular verse. The verse whose first letters form this month's letter sequence is from the Book of *Yirmiyahu* / Jeremiah (9:23): ***Y**is-halel…**H**a-mishalel **H**a-maskil **V**'yade'a* / Let he that glories, glory in this: that he understands and knows (Me). This verse focuses on *Hasagah* (a type of 'intellectual awareness') and *Binah* / understanding.

In general, there are 50 'gates' of Binah; 49 levels of understanding that we can climb, and a 50th level that can only be granted as a gift from Above (*Rosh Hashanah*, 21b. *Nedarim*, 38a). This is the deeper reason why, during this time of year, we count the 49 days between Pesach and Shavuos, then on the 50th day we cease counting and receive the gift of Torah.*

This period between Pesach and Shavuos is called *Sefiras haOmer* / Counting the Omer Offering. *Sefiras haOmer* stretches over three separate months. It begins on the second day of Pesach in the middle of Nisan, extends throughout the whole month of Iyyar, and concludes on the day before Shavuos in the beginning of Sivan. Iyyar is thus the only month which is completely dedicated to, and therefore defined by the Counting of the Omer. Iyyar is therefore understood as a time of rebuilding and refining the foundations of our Binah.

The kind of *Hasagah* / perception that becomes more readily available during the month of Iyyar is a heightened sensitivity to the deeper meanings and rhythms of time. This expanded awareness is achieved and expressed through the Counting of the Omer, a spiritual practice we will explore in great depth throughout the following pages. Suffice it to say for now, *Sefiras haOmer* is a practice of counting each day, or put another way, of making each day count. Specifically, the practice is such: each night, starting on the second day of Pesach until and including the day before Shavuos, we say a blessing and subsequently count the day, from one to forty-nine. In addition to the blessing and the counting of each day, we also correlate each day to a set of interincluded *Sefirotic* energies, moving downward from *Chesed* to *Malchus*. The combination of blessing, counting, and correlating each day is a kind of cumulative practice

---

* There is an allusion to this in the fact that the word *Torah* (in the singular form) appears in the Torah 50 times (*Rokeach*, on Devarim 6:7).

that connects the liberation of Pesach to the revelation of Shavuos.

As it is influenced by and focused on a specific set of psycho-spiritual qualities, each day of the month of Iyyar introduces a new form or approach to our *Avodah* / spiritual-mental-emotional 'work.' When that day's work has been completed, we move forth to the next day's focus, sweeping through the seven lower *Sefiros* seven separate times over a period of seven weeks. Each week we refine one of our seven psycho-emotional attributes in seven different ways, all in preparation to receive the Torah on the fiftieth day, which is Shavuos.

Time itself is a manifestation of *Din* or separation. The basic construct of past, present, and future is one of *Din*, as it is based on individually distinct units or segments. Iyyar's sharp separation between days — as we are counting each day, and adopting different forms of *Avodah* for each day — is an intense expression of *Din*. And yet, counting is also an expression of *Chesed*, unification, or integration. You cannot count day 'two' (*Din)* if you did not first count 'one' — one is included inseparably within two. In this way, the counting actually unifies all of the numbers. For example, when you count today as day 20, you are unifying all 19 preceding days into the 20th day. Thus, as represented in this month's permutation of the Divine Name, Iyyar is a month that is focused on achieving a healthy balance and fruitful coexistence of the necessary qualities of *Chesed* and *Din*.

LETTER

According to the Sefer Yetzirah, there are three types of letters in the Aleph Beis: three 'mother' letters, seven 'double' letters, and twelve 'simple' letters. Each month of the year is connected with one of the twelve 'simple' letters.

The letter of the month of Iyyar is Vav (ו). Vav is a symbol of connection and continuity (*Pesachim*, 5a), as the letter Vav can mean 'and' when added to the beginning of a word. Also, as a word in itself, Vav means 'a hook,' a connector or unifier (*Shemos*, 26:32). Iyyar, as the second month, is a 'connecting month,' creating the connection and continuity between Nisan and Sivan ("And you shall make fifty loops" *Shemos*, 26:10, corresponds to the 50 days that connects Pesach with Shavuos. Rabbeinu Ephrayim, see, *Chomas Anach*, Terumah, 8). Nisan is the month of redemption, and on the first day of Sivan begins the process of the giving of the Torah (*Shabbos*, 86b). Thus Iyyar connects redemption with revelation.

Alternatively, in Nisan we are spiritually like newborns, and in the third month of Sivan we reach maturity and receive the Torah. Between babyhood and maturity is a time of childhood and adolescence. In Iyyar we connect these two states, infancy and maturity, by focusing on 'growing up.' Like youngsters, we too may be brimming with emotions during this time, and perhaps dealing with feelings of aggression or stubbornness. The work of self-refinement in the face of these sentiments creates a strong bond, connecting the wide-eyed wonder of being 'new' (Nisan) to the groundedness, focus, and balance of maturity (Sivan).

We see this idea of Iyyar being a month of connection reflected in practical *Halacha* / law. There is a custom brought down in *Shulchan Aruch* / Table of Laws which is conceptually relevant (Rema, Even Ezra, 126:7): one should not divorce during the month of Iyyar. The simple reason given is that there is a debate about whether Iyyar is written with one Yud or two. We can also say there is also a deeper reason: the energy of Iyyar is characterized by the letter Vav, meaning connectivity, and therefore no severing of spouses should take place in Iyyar. The idea of 'separation' does come into play during this month, but it is a separation that increases connection, as we will explore.

Graphically, the letter Vav is a line, representing linear time, from past to present to future. It also represents linear causality, connecting cause and effect. Vav has a numerical value of six, representing the six days of the work-week prior to Shabbos. During these six days, we prepare for Shabbos in a linear fashion; progressing one day at a time, moving towards and connecting to Shabbos. In the same way, during Iyyar, we count the days of the Omer period, from one to forty-nine, preparing and anticipating the experience of the Giving of the Torah on Shavuos.

Iyyar is an acronym for Avraham, Yitzchak, Ya'akov, and Rachel (Ya'akov's primary wife) (*Beis Shemuel*, Even Ezra, *Siman* 126:7). Avraham is the first name in the acronym, as he too is also connected to Iyyar (*Pesikta Rabsi*, Parsha 28:5).* These four personalities, and the energies they represent, are called the Secret of the *Merkava* / Divine Chariot (*Haga'as Rabbi Akiva Eiger*, ibid). The nature of the Divine *Merkava* is that it connects Above with below, Heaven to earth. This is another reference within the word *Iyyar* to connectivity, as represented by the *Vav*.

Healing, which is a result of alignment and proper connectivity between soul and body (between functions and organs of the body itself), is also part of the quality of Iyyar, as will be explored in the following section.

---

*One subtle connection between Avraham and Iyyar is that he ran to get a calf (a young bull) to serve his guests (*Bereishis*, 18:7). The astrological sign for Iyyar is the Bull. *Pesikta Rabsi*, Parsha 28:5.

NAME OF THE MONTH

Each month of the twelve months of the year has a distinct name, and every name has a meaning. According to our sages, the current names we have for the months were imported to our tradition upon our return to Israel from the Babylonian Exile. They can in fact be traced to ancient Babylonian or Akkadian names (*Yerushalmi*, Rosh Hashanah, 1:2. *Medrash Rabbah*, Bereishis, 48:9). In the times before the Babylonian Exile, the names of the months were mostly known by their number in the sequence of the year. For example, the month of Av was called the Fifth Month, and Cheshvan was known as the Eighth Month.

Before the Babylonian Exile Iyyar was called *Ziv*/ray or brightness, because the sun's brightness intensifies significantly during this month. *Ziv* is also the name the Torah itself uses for this month

(*Melachim* I, 6:3. *Rosh Hashanah*, 11a, *Rashi* ad loc.). 'Brightness' refers to the beginning of spring, and thus Nisan, the first month of the spring, is also called *Ziv* (*Tosefos*, Rosh Hashanah, 2b.) After the Babylonian Exile, however, our sages began to use the name Iyyar. This name is related to the word *Yirah* / fear or awe. The name *Ziv* is more an expression of *Chesed* / Divine kindness, whereas the name Iyyar is more an expression of *Din* or *Gevurah*. Taken together, these two names again point to the complex combination of judgment, separation, and longing present in this month, juxtaposed with the sense of deep unity, connection, and kindness.

There is an argument among sages (*Yerushalmi*, *Rosh Hashanah*, 1:2. *Medrash Rabbah*, Bereishis, 48:9. *Tosefos*, Rosh Hashanah 7a. Even Ezra, Ramban, Chezkuni, Shemos. 12:2. Bnei Yissaschar, Nisan, Ma'amor 1:6. Divrei Torah, (Munkatch) Mahadurah 2:7), whether or not the names for the months that we have today are derived from Torah names — are they Hebrew names that were lost over time and later rediscovered, or names that were borrowed from other peoples by the end of the Babylonian Exile? If the name Iyyar was borrowed from another culture, it seems to have come from the word *Ayaru*, the Canaanite name for the same month. *Ayaru*, just like *Ziv*, means 'bright.'

Breaking the word down into letters, we see that Iyyar is an acronym for *Ani Hashem Rofecha* / "I am Hashem your healer" (*Shemos*, 15:26. *Chasam Sofer*, Shabbos, 147b. *Pri Tzadik*, Iyyar). Based on this and other considerations, which we will now explore, our sages teach that Iyyar is a month of healing (*Shabbos*, 147b). Indeed, R. Shimon Bar Yochai, the protagonist and hero of the month of Iyyar, is himself connected to healing. His name, Shimon Bar Yochai, in numerical terms is 703, same as the word ורפאתי / "and I (Hashem) will heal him" (*Yeshayahu*, 57:19). Furthermore, R. Pinchas of Kortez teaches that if a person needs to start a prescription or regiment of medicine, he should begin it in the month of Iyyar (*Imrei Pinchas*, 231).

According to our sages, one reason why Iyyar is connected to healing is that the sunlight increases and sunlight brings healing (*Nedarim*, 10a). Along these lines, it could be said that Iyyar is a month of healing simply because of natural reasons, such as the increasing warmth and sunlight. Yet, the truth is that everything on the physical plane is a manifestation and projection of the spiritual plane. The healing energy of Iyyar is fundamentally metaphysical, yet it is expressed and manifest through the healing sunlight of the month.

IYYAR AND THE NUMBER EIGHT

We have been primarily speaking of Iyyar as the second month of the year starting from Nisan, however, Iyyar is also the eighth month of the solar year beginning with Tishrei on Rosh Hashanah. The number eight is conceptually bound to the idea of healing. Our sages tell us that the reason the eighth blessing in the *Amidah* / the silent standing prayer is about healing, is because the *Bris* / circumcision occurs on the eighth day of a boy's life, this ritual requires healing (*Megillah*, 16b). For the male newborn, the Bris could be, and hopefully is, the first wound, as it were, that needs healing.

When we visit a sick person on Shabbos we declare, "It is Shabbos, and we should not cry out; healing will soon arrive" (*Shabbos*, 12a). The phrase, "will soon arrive," hints to the fact that on the seventh day, we can easily access the adjacent paradigm of ultimate healing, which is 'eight.'

Most weaknesses and illnesses come from eating food that is not consistent with our needs and body type (*Bnei Yissaschar*, Iyyar, Ma'amar 1:3). The *Mon* / Manna, however, was a food that nourished and healed each person according to their individual needs. Iyyar is the month when the Mon began to descend in the desert (*Shemos*, 16:1-4), and this event left an indelible imprint on the month. The healing effects of the Mon can be subtly felt in the body even today, and especially during the month of Iyyar.

Three Types of Healing

Ultimate healing is associated with the number eight, but there are different types of healing connected with 'six' and 'seven' as well. Acquiring a better understanding of each of these individual types of healing will help us achieve a deeper and more detailed understanding of healing in general.

Six — Linear Healing

'Six' is symbolized by the letter Vav, a line, and therefore represents linear time. Healing within the 'six' paradigm is linear, meaning it is ruled by the principle of causality. Here, if you cut your hand, you must bandage it to stop the bleeding and keep it protected. Here, 'healing' means to change an already existing injury or illness. The letter Vav also means "and", Vav is a connector.

In the paradigm of 'six,' healing is dependent on linear connections — between doctors and patients, between symptoms and causes, between diagnoses and medicines.

Seven — Circular Healing

The Seventh Day, the completion of the natural cycle, represents 'circle' energy, or causeless perfection without beginning or end. Healing from the level of 'seven' is the healing of Shabbos, the paradigm of 'circles.' In this form of healing, one realizes that everything is already perfect and whole, no matter what state it seems to be in on the surface. Bleeding may or may not stop in this state of transcendent wholeness, but either way, the situation is deeply accepted as perfect. Although an actual outcome does not matter to us in this state, the unconditional positivity of acceptance is itself a state of health. Since 'seven' includes 'six' positivity and peace can also help cause healing on the physical, linear level. Simply having an unconditionally positive attitude about life — a Shabbos perspective — our minds affect our body, and thus can tremendously affect our overall health for the better.

Eight — Spiral Healing

'Six' is the days of the week, and the directions of space. Shabbos is the midpoint within this six, the center and core of natural reality, the point of perfection within the cycle of time. 8, however, represents the complete transcendence of the natural world. 'Eight' signifies the quality of *Shomer haHekef* / the protective circumference surrounding the natural world (*Teshuvas haRashba* I, Teshuvah 9). This hints to the idea of *Makif* / The surrounding or transcendent reality. The Maharal teaches that 'eight' signifies the miraculous —

that which transcends nature — as in the miraculous eight days of Chanukah. It is important to note that the miracles of Chanukah included an element of human participation and effort, and this relates to eight's inclusion and unification of 'seven' and 'six,' as we will shortly explain.

'Eight' is not a simple transcendence like Shabbos, whence we purely transcend work and illness. In the paradigm of eight, we actively participate in the linear healing process; while we simultaneously recognize that everything is perfect as it is. 'Eight' is a paradox, at once representing nature and the transcendence of nature. It is the unity of the 'line' paradigm of 'doing' and the 'circle' paradigm of 'being.' It is a paradoxical combination of causality and non-causality, multiplicity and non-duality; we do what is necessary to bring healing, yet we accept the perfection of what is, simultaneously enlisting and submitting our will in recognition that it is Hashem who is the only healer.

The number eight is mentioned explicitly in relation to the Mitzvah of circumcision on the eighth day of a boy's life (*Bereishis*, 21:4). In circumcision, the 'line' of the male organ is circumcised and the foreskin is removed, leaving an *Atara* or 'crown' — which is a circle. We see in this a visceral metaphor for the way in which eight both transcends and includes the paradigms of six and seven.

The Torah also mentions that, "On the eighth day (of the dedication period), the Mishkan was established." The *Mishkan* / Nomadic Sanctuary in the desert, was a microcosm of creation in its entirety and the dwelling place of the Divine. We see here again the concept of 'eight' representing active human participation in the completion and fulfilment of Hashem's universe.

Hashem creates the world in six days and rests on the seventh; the Divine creative work is complete in the paradigm of 'seven.' The human role, however, is to add an additional level of 'completion' to Hashem's world, in the mode of 'eight.' We are meant to participate in the Creation of the world so we can refine ourselves. Hashem says, "I created the world *l'Takkein* / to make a *Tikkun* / Repair (Bereishis, 2:3, *Rashi* from *Medrash*). In other words, 'Your actions can repair and improve My world.' Tikkun specifically comes about through the mode of 'eight,' the unification of worldly action and Heavenly acceptance. We human beings have a Divine charge to 'improve' upon Hashem's creation by making a circumcision on the eighth day, and establishing the Mishkan on the eighth day. The Mitzvah of Circumcision represents the inner work that we must do on ourselves, while the Mishkan represents our calling in the world.

Our sages tell a story of Turnus Rufus, who once asked the great sage Rabbi Akiva, "Whose deeds are greater, those of the Creator or those of people?" Intuiting that Turnus Rufus's question was really 'Why do you circumcise yourselves?' Rabbi Akiva answered, "Those of people are greater." He then brought out stalks of grain, symbolizing that which is made by the Creator, and beautiful baked cakes, symbolizing that which is made by people. He asked Turnus Rufus which was greater. "Yes," Turnus Rufus replied, "but if the Creator wants you to be circumcised, why aren't you born circumcised?" Rabbi Akiva asked, "Why does an infant's umbilical cord have to be cut after birth? We are not born circumcised because the Mitzvos were given to refine us." (*Tanchuma*, Tazria-Metzora).

There was once a woman whose son was ill, and to elicit Divine help she circumambulated the *Azara* / courtyard surrounding the *Beis haMikdash* / Holy Temple (*S'machos*, Chap. 6). It is brought down that since today there is no Azara or Holy Temple, the custom is to walk around the *Teivah* / box or *Bima* upon which the Torah is read in the synagogue. (R. Yoseph Caro speaks of circling, seven times, the gravesites of Tzadikim to ward off all negative decrees. *Magid Mesharim*, Parshas Emor). The optimum practice is that the sick person circle the Teivah, but if this is not feasible, a family member may do it on his or her behalf. When the person circles the *Teivah* (some sources suggest seven times) he should pray for healing, and those observing should also pray. Some have a tradition to recite, as they circle, the verse that includes the words that Moshe prayed when his sister Miriam was struck with an ailment: "And Moshe cried out to Hashem, saying, *E-l Na, Refa Na La* / 'Please G-d, please heal her!' (*Bamidbar*, 12:13). Others have a tradition (*Shu't Divrei Yitzchak*, R. Yitzchak Kaduri, p. 407), that before each of the seven circumambulations, one should recite one of the seven verses from the *Ana b'Koach* prayer, and meditate on the corresponding Sefirah from the seven Sefiros.

The blessing of this healing procedure emanates, in a sense, through the Torah that is placed on the Bima. The Torah scroll itself embodies the unification of Vav (six) and Zayin (seven), as it is inscribed with lines and yet rolled as a circle, into a scroll. With the receiving of the Divine Torah on Mount Sinai, all illness and even mortality were momentarily removed from the world. This occurred on the 50th day of the Omer, alluding to the level of eight, the next step beyond the seven cycles of seven days.

When the person circles the Bima seven times, and does so with intention as well as attention, they enter into the place of eight, as it were, unifying the 'box' or cube of 'six' and the circle of 'seven' in order to stimulate a flow of healing. This physical act - G-d willing - triggers a spiritual reaction Above, drawing down Divine flow, that unifies spiritual perfection with the experience of physical 'imperfection' or illness below. This can allow a total healing of body and soul to manifest.

Ultimate healing is thus rooted in the paradigm of eight, the space of inclusive-transcendence. This is connected to the world of *Keser* / Divine crown. Keser is also called *Arich Anpin* / Long Face. Iyyar is numerically 221, which is the same as the word *Arich* (Aleph/1 + Reish/200 + Chaf/20 = 221). The Torah is the meta-root of creation; anything and everything of this world is rooted within the Torah, healing included. The specific root of healing is in the words of the Torah: *Ki Ani Hashem Rofecha* / "for I am Hashem Your Healer" (*Shemos*, 15:26). All healing originates in these sacred words. The first letters of these four words spell the word *Arich* (see, Tzemach Tzedek, *Yahel Ohr*, *Tehilim* 6:1). All modes of healing — the causal mode of 'six' and the non-causal mode of 'seven' — are rooted in the level of 8, the inclusive-transcendence of *Arich*, which is gematria Iyyar.

SENSE

The sense or skill corresponding to this month is *Hirhur*, a subtle type of intelligence. *Hirhur* means subtle thought, alluding to a deep sense of inner hearing. This quality of *Hirhur* is uniquely human — whereas all the other 'senses,' like sleeping, tasting, and walking, (even perhaps laughter, as found in monkeys), (although see Ya'avetz, *Mitpachas Sefarim*, 8:8), are functions that are also found throughout the animal kingdom (The Gra, *Sefer Yetzirah*, 5:2). As such, the whole idea of the Sefirah period is moving from a state of animal consciousness, symbolized by the *Omer* / barley offering, which was considered animal food at the time, to a more fully human consciousness, represented by the *Shtei haLechem*, the wheat offerings on Shavuos, which was considered the archetypal human food (see Maharal, *Tiferes Yisrael*, chap. 25. The Rema, *Toras haOlah*, 3:54). This form of intelligence and wisdom includes an exceptionally perceptive awareness of time, and a heightened sensitivity to the meaningful rhythms of both season and soul.

According to the Geonim version of the *Sefer Yetzirah*, which is subtly different than the system we generally follow throughout this text, the month of Nisan is connected with the sense of sight, while the month of Iyyar is connected with the sense of hearing. Sight is a unified or simultaneous power— it is virtually timeless, or miraculous as it were, allowing us to view an entire picture in a single moment. The sense of hearing is linear or gradual, requiring us to absorb information one unit at a time. In Nisan, we see the truth instantaneously, as a gift from Above. To sustain this vision, however, we have to bring it down into the world of hearing, or in other words, into the vessels of time and process. That's why in Iyyar we do not overtly celebrate any miraculous or timeless events, but each day of this month has a special Mitzvah for us to perform, a unique form of *Avodah* / spiritual work. As we count the days of the Omer throughout Iyyar, we also meditate upon the Seven Sefiros / the basic emotional attributes one-by-one. We use these Sefiros as a template for self-investigation and a guide for our work in 'bringing down' the inspiration and gifts we received in Nisan and making them sustainable and real in our everyday life.

As we gradually prepare ourselves for the holiday of Shavuos, the day we receive the Torah, by counting each day of the Omer along with its unique Sefirotic correspondence, it would seem to make sense to start from the bottom of the Sefirotic Tree and work our way up, from *Malchus* / Receptivity (the lowest of the seven attributes) to *Chesed* / Kindness and giving (the highest of the seven Sefiros). Then the 50th day would be *Binah* / Divine Understanding, alluding to a realm of freedom above Chesed and all of the other reactive emotions. So why in fact do we count from *Chesed* down to *Malchus*?

The celebrated Chassidic Rebbe, the Shem Mishmuel writes that as a child he asked his father, the Avnei Nezer, this very question. And his father responded that we count downward because it is easier to create a *Tikkun* / rectification and realignment on the higher emotional attributes (*Shem Mishmuel*, Rosh Hashanah, p. 28). Perhaps, this is because the higher emotions are more linked to *Mochin* / higher intellect and thus contain more of a quality of 'mind over matter,' and a propensity to be more proactive than reactive. In any case, whenever we are aspiring to create *Tikkun* and working to perfect a certain negative pattern of behavior, we need to start with what is easier to rectify, and proceed to what is more difficult. We build on our successes; each success breeds more success and increases our power and confidence to be increasingly successful in the future.

SIGN

Shor / the bull (Tauros) is the astrological sign of the month (see also *Rashi, Baba Metziya*, 106b). This animal is a symbol of brute power (*Mishlei*, 14:4), and of our inner qualities of aggressive strength, stubbornness, simplicity, self-confidence, and emotional volatility. Iyyar is the month of Taurus because it is the second month of the spring, which is a time when our self-assurance and assertiveness are naturally stimulated, as discussed previously. The bull is also a symbol of the 'left side' (*Yechezkel* 1:10), which is the aspect of *Gevurah* / strength, severity, and separation. As mentioned, Iyyar is characterized as a time of Gevurah.

In general, the bull is a symbol of the *Yetzer haRa* (*Keheles Ya'akov*

Oys Shin, Shor. Note, *Avodah Zara*, 5b.), which also corresponds to the 'left side.' Taurus is considered a 'dark' sign (Rabbeinu Bachya, *Kad Kemach*, Rosh Hashanah 2), intrinsically connected to 'darkness' (*Pesikta Rabbasi*, Parsha 19:2). In fact, the Hebrew word *Shor* / bull is an acronym for *Soneh* / despised, ***v'Tamei*** / and impure, ***Ra*** / bad. All of these terms are references to the *Yetzer haRa* / the negative inclination (see, *Sukkah*, 52a), otherwise referred to as the animal soul. However, as the Prophet says, "The bull knows its master" (*Yeshayahu*, 1:3). In other words, the bull may be stubborn, but it is ultimately aligned with the Master of the Universe. Even 'bull-headedness' and aggression may be harnessed for wholesome acts of goodness and kindness if properly channeled.

Those born under the sign of Shor are people who look for stability, security, and control. They may prefer to be self-employed and they may own property. Additionally, they can be overly self-protective or possessive. Their desire for stability can make them more stubborn and can lead to arrogance, yet, this desire to stabilize can also produce gifts of healing, integration, and realignment.

At a crucial point in Jewish history, during the counting of the Omer, the students of the great first century sage Rabbi Akiva were dying en masse (the extreme opposite of healing). Tradition ascribes the cause of their death to their not showing respect for one another, and that they were overly aggressive with their own convictions. Because of this, the Omer period became a time dedicated to working on ourselves and gaining some measure of self-mastery over our emotions. (This story, which is one of the signature stories used to contemplate the deeper meanings of the Omer period, will be explored in depth throughout the following sections.)

The month of Iyyar contains no Torah festivals or Rabbinic holidays; meaning there is no specific flow of blessings from Above to help us during this time. Self-work is the only available vehicle for spiritual progress in Iyyar. This is also why during this period we study *Pirkei Avos* / Ethics of our Ancestors, a collection of teachings from our sages that help us become more attentive to our behavior, and aware of its repercussions. As a result of this focus and work on refining our unconscious-emotional response-patterns during the month of Iyyar, from Counting the Omer to studying *Pirkei Avos*, we can hopefully learn to contain the aggressive, self-involved power of our internal 'bull,' redirect that raw energy toward positivity, and align our character traits with holiness.

TRIBE

Yisachar / Issachar is the tribe associated with the month of Iyyar. The tribe of Yisachar developed a deep understanding and sensitivity to the nature and rhythms of time."*U'bnei Yisachar Yodea Binah l'Itim* / And the Children of Yisachar know the wisdom of time" (*Divrei haYamim* I, 12:32. Yuma, 26a). What this rather cryptic statement means is that they knew the secrets of *Ibur* / pregnancy (referring to leap years, when a year needs to be impregnated with a 13th month), *Shanim* / years (referring to the solar count), and how to establish the dates of *Roshei Chodashim* / Heads of new months (referring to the lunar count) (*Esther Rabbah*, 1).

Beyond this heightened sensitivity to the subtle mechanics of time, they also possessed the functional wisdom and acumen to 'unify' all of the individual days, months, seasons, and celestial cycles into a single, seamless, integrated calendar.

The period of Sefiras haOmer introduces us to a similar sensitivity to both the rhythms of time, as well as the unification of time. As we count the days of the Omer we internalize the understanding that today we can only count 'day six' if yesterday we counted 'day five.' Such is the nature of counting; every number is a unique and separate entity, but to proceed to the next number we need all the previous ones together. When we count 'six,' we include and unify the previous five counts, and when we finally reach 50, we have unified all the cycles and qualities of the entire Omer period. To illustrate this dynamic we can look at the traditional wording of the Omer count. The colloquial way of counting days would be to say, "Today is *Yom Sheini* / the second day" or "Today is *Yom Chamishi* / the fifth day." The way we count during the Omer is, "Today is *Shnei Yamim* / two days," "Today is *Chamishah Yamim* / five days." By doing so, we are always including the previous days in our counting of the present moment. Our counting thus has a cumulative, unifying effect.

At the end, we take all the individual units of time, and compile them together as a single unit, bridging the liberation of Pesach and the revelation of Shavuos. We thus unify our birth as a people with our maturation and reception of our collective purpose.

Associated with the word *Sefirah* is the word *Sefar* / edge, as in the edge of a city, implying a boundary or defined space. This is also the nature of counting. We count defined individual units, distinct days with their different qualities. On the other hand, whenever we count something, there is a sum total, a *Sach haKol* / final count, which unifies all the individual units into a singular whole that is greater than the sum of its parts. The coincidence of holistic singularity and multiple individual units suggests a transparent or illuminated medium, such as *Sappir* / Sapphire or luminary (see *Shemos*, 24:10 and 28:18. *Zohar Chadash*, Yisro, 41b. *Zohar 2*, 136b). *Sappir*, parenthetically, is another word related to *Sefirah*. This coincidence of unity and multiplicity suggests that all numbers are pointing to something beyond counting, beyond the world of separation, to a transparent, luminous, singular wholeness.

In the counting of the 49 days of the Omer, we are moving towards the 50th day, at which time we receive the Torah anew. The number 50 is also connected to the *Yovel* / the Jubilee year, which is the paradigm of freedom, both spiritually and socially. When we received the Torah we became truly 'free' (*Avos*, 6:2), and even immortal i.e., free from the angel of death (*Medrash Rabbah*, Shemos, 41). The number 50 represents a step beyond multiplicity into the world of infinite oneness. Through the counting of individual units, we reach a place beyond individuality and quantification, as the Prophet says regarding Klal Yisrael, "And the *Mispar* / number of the People of Israel shall be as the sand of the sea, which *cannot* be …counted" (*Hoshea* 2:1). In other words, the number indicates a reality beyond enumeration.

Throughout the period of *Sefiras haOmer*, we move from the realm of '49' finite digits, into the world of infinite oneness, freedom, and transparency (*Ohr HaChayim*, 23:15) — the world of 50.

Regarding the Torah it says, "ארכה מארץ מדה ורחבה מני ים" / "Longer than the earth is its measure (*Midah*), and wider than the sea (*Yam*)" (*Iyov*, 11:9). The word *Midah* / measure, has a numerical value of 49 (*Megalah Amukos*, Parshas Behar. In an earlier source, *Sefer Rokeach*, Hilchos Pesach, 294). Deep beyond the measurable natural world is the level of 50, the numerical value of the word *Yam* / sea.

BODY PART

The month of Iyyar is associated with the right kidney. Our sages teach that the kidneys give *Eitzah* / advice (*Berachos*, 61a). Rashi writes that the source for this is *Tehilim* / Psalms (16:7) — "Even at night my kidneys advise me." Our kidneys thus symbolize our ability to discern good from bad, and the right kidney expressly symbolizes choosing the good (Maharsha, *ad loc*). The 'advice' of the kidneys is specifically related to self-refinement, and especially within a context of night, which alludes to a time of *Din* / harsh judgment, separation, and constricted flow. Each day of the Omer, which we count at night, conveys a specific piece of spiritual advice, based on the combination of *Sefiros* and character traits of the day. By counting each day throughout Iyyar and the Omer period, which, as discussed, is a time of *Din*, we are tapping into our kidneys, so to speak, in order to access inner guidance as we progress along the path of self-transformation, which lies between the liberation of Nisan and the revelation of Sivan.

Hair may not be a 'body part' per se, but it is significant to discuss in this context since the *Rishonim* / Early Commentators, including Rabbeinu Yerucham *(Toldas Adam,* Nesiv 5:4. *Derisha,* Orach Chayim, 493:1), advise us not to cut our hair during the Omer period. This is because hair embodies *Din,* separation, and constricted flow.* We could therefore ask, should it not be the other way around — should we not cut our Din away during this time? Perhaps we should cut our hair every single day of the Omer; why should we let our hair grow and add on to the *Din*?

Hair condenses, funnels, and transmits energy in a narrow stream. Paralleling the cosmic structure, every strand of thin, linear hair on one's head represents a flow of *Din* / constriction and limitation, a finely condensed flow of light. Each strand of hair grows individually. There are no two hairs that occupy one follicle *(Niddah,* 52b. See also *Shaloh HaKodesh,* Sha'ar haOsyos, Os Kuf, Kedusha 2). And yet, depending on the style and length, these individual hairs can also be made to appear as one single flowing entity. Hair thus represents both individuality and multiplicity.

---

* Some of the Rishonim (Rabbeinu Yerucham. *Toldos Adam,* Nesiv 5:4) write that the time of the Omer is a time of Din, as *Se'or* / barley, the offering of 'animal food' on the altar, represents Din — and this is why we do not cut our *Se'ir* / hair during this period. Rabbi Moshe Dovid Valle writes (*Sefer HaLikutim* 2, p. 553) that since head hair is Din, and beard hair is Chesed / kindness and giving, we grow them both during this time of Din; the head hair to allow Din, as it is a time of Din (and we need to accept and honor Din when it is a time of Din, as will be explored further on), and the beard hair to sweeten the judgments of Din.

Closely-cut hair reveals more of the separate individuality of each strand; the closer to the scalp, the more recognizable each individual hair. Shorter hair therefore represents judgment, law, and order. The *Cohen* / Priest served in the Beis haMikdash with very short hair (*Bamidbar* 8:7. *Tannis*, 17b). His service was replete with routine and order, including a daily offering in the morning and a daily offering in the evening.

Unlike the Cohen who represents order and routine, the *Nazir* is one who chooses to live a life of *Pelah* / wonder, transcendence, and radical unity. The Nazir's commitment to expansive consciousness is represented by his ritually uncut hair. Uncut or long hair flows more smoothly like a single integrated entity, and it thus has a more unified nature. This type of hair is a combination of individuality and collectivity.

This paradox of individuality and collectivity, as demonstrated in uncut hair, relates to the month of Iyyar — a month of *Din*, individuality, multiplicity, separation and self-expression, and at the same time a month of *Chesed*, 'healing' or expansion into integration, alignment, and unification. Ultimately, the highest form of healing is to bring unity and wholeness down into the 'multiple' details of our lives. This again, is the paradigm of 'eight' — that which unifies the 'six' of *Din* (multiplicity) and the 'seven' of *Chesed* (unity).*

---

*Keser is the Sefirah that includes both individuality and multiplicity. The time of the Omer is connected to Rabbi Akiva. He is also connected with Chochmah, and beyond, to the 50th level, which is Keser (and also connected to Binah). That is why he is *Doresh Tagim* / pursuing the meanings in the crowns on the letters, which are beyond the upper tips of the letters. The Yud-like tips of the letters represent Chochmah and the Tagim which rise above their level represent Keser. This is the inner reason why we do not cut our hair during Sefirah, as our hair is also rooted in Keser, the crown which rests above our seat of Chochmah, the brain (see: *Bnei Yissaschar,* Nisan 12:8).

ELEMENT

Iyyar is associated with the element of *Afar* / Earth. The element of earth is cold and dry. Although it occurs in a warmer time of year, Iyyar has a spiritual coldness and dryness to it as there are no Torah based or even Rabbinic Holidays during the month; Lag b'Omer is technically 'post-Rabbinic,' and as such is not considered a true 'holiday.' Iyyar is a month in which our growth toward Divine intimacy is motivated by a sense of distance. This is similar to the time of *Niddah* / the 'menstrual period' during which spouses are not physically intimate, in marriage relationships. This separation creates a deeper longing to connect. (This comparison of Iyyar and the *Niddah* period will be explored in more depth in Part 2.)

The 'earthy' quality of the month means that it is a month of 'grounded' and gradual inner work. Iyyar is not a time of Heavenly fires, splitting seas or Divine inspirations, Iyyar is a time of self-motivated, detail-oriented, day-to-day soul tilling. It is a month in which we harness the liberatory energy from Nisan and anchor it in the practical world, one day at a time. Through counting and working on ourselves each day of Iyyar, we bring another facet of the exalted light and freedom of Pesach down to earth. This gradual process of patiently integrating liberation brings us closer to the revelation of Sinai with every step.

TORAH PORTIONS

The Torah portions of this month are, in many ways, concerned with identifying meaningful rhythms of time, understanding the attribute and mechanisms of Din in our lives, and participating in the process of purification and preparation to re-enter communal and ritual life on a higher level.

Parshas Tazria-Metzorah discusses numerous laws of *Tumah* / spiritual stagnancy, detailing how individuals could become temporarily isolated or stagnant in their lives, and constricted in a halachic and ritual sense, by means of certain lifecycle events. All forms of *Tumah* are connected with various degrees of death or contact with death.

Acharei Mos and Kedoshim speak of the events and laws given following the death of the sons of Aaron.

Emor discusses Tumah, as above, and *Taharah* / the purification process, how one receives healing and integration following bouts with Tumah.

Behar speaks of the cycles of the *Shemitah* and *Yovel* years, which are cycles of seven and of 50 years, respectively. This is similar to the cycle of seven weeks of the Omer and the 50th day of Shavuos.

Bechukosai expresses Divine judgment in the form of rebukes. The 33rd day of the Omer, Lag b'Omer, always falls around the week in which we read Bechukosai, in Bechukosai the Torah elaborates 33 blessings and also 33 'rebukes'. (*Beis Ya'akov* [Ishbitz], Parshas Bechukosai). Bechukosai is the 33rd portion of the Torah. Additionally, in the first verse of Bechukosai, there are 33 letters.

SEASON OF THE YEAR

We will explore the subject of the time of year and the 'holiday' of the month, at length in "Part Two: Lag b'Omer." Here, in preparation for those future considerations, we will delve into a few major aspects of the spiritual psychology of the season of spring, in which Iyyar occurs.

During this second month of spring, as the weather warms and we begin to acclimate to the awakening world around us, it is natural to go outside and interact more with others. In Nisan we had already completed and broken out of the insular mode of winter 'hibernation,' but we were still too occupied with preparing our homes for Pesach to spend much time outdoors. The expansive outward movement of Iyyar lends itself to assertive self-expression, which in turn can lead toward arrogance or impulsiveness.

This predominance of self-assertiveness and the impulsive need to express oneself helps explain a perplexing event in history; an event which is considered fundamental to understanding the energy of Iyyar and the entire Omer period. We are told that the great sage Rabbi Akiva had 24,000 students* and all of them died during the Omer period,** "Because they did not conduct themselves with *Kavod* / respect towards one another...they all died between Pesach and Shavuos" (*Yevamos*, 62b).

This story is quite puzzling on many levels. For instance, is it possible that the students of Rabbi Akiva — the sage who famously taught, "Loving your fellow as yourself is the primary principle of the Torah" (*Sifra* 2) — did not respect each other, and even begrudged each other (*Medrash Rabbah*, Bereishis, 61:3)?***

The answer is that love does not necessarily translate into respect (Lubavitcher Rebbe, *Likutei Sichos*, 7. p. 342). In fact, Rabbi Akiva's

---

* Twenty-four thousand students in all, which wousld be 12,000 'pairs' of students (*Medrash Rabbah*, Bereishis, 61:3. *Koheles Rabbah* 11. *Yalkut Shimoni*, Koheles 989). Yet, the Gemarah in Nedarim (50a) speaks of Rabbi Akiva having 24,000 pairs of students, which would be 48,000 students total. The *Tanchuma* (Chayei Sara, 6) tells us that Rabbi Akiva had 300 students. Yet, we know that in *Chazal* / writings of the sages the number 300 is not meant literally, rather it represents a large or exaggerated number (*Teshuvas, Mahara M'panu. Mei HaShiluach* 1, Noach. See also *Rashbam*, Pesachim 119a. *Rashi*, Chulin, 90b).

** The 24,000 students of Rabbi Akiva who died were *Gilgulim* / reincarnations of the people of *Shechem*. After the incident with Dina, 24,000 of the people of *Shechem* were killed, and were initially reincarnated into the tribe of Shimon. Then, in that first *Gilgul*, they were killed in the plague at *Shittim*, after the incident with the *B'nos Moav* / daughters of Moab and Zimri. They finally reached their *Tikkun* through incarnating as the 24,000 students of Rabbi Akiva who died (*Sefer Gilgulim. Megaleh Amukos*, 86. See *Sheim m'Shmuel*, Hagadah, on *Sefirah*). The word *Moav*, incidentally, has a numerical value of 49, alluding to the Omer.

*** Perhaps his 24,000 students did not learn from him the art of *Kavod*/Respect, because Rabbi Akiva gathered them together when he was living alone, without a wife or children (*Kesubos*, 62b-63a), and Kavod is learned by example. His students therefore couldn't observe how he would treat his wife and children with the utmost care and respect, during all those years that they were separated. This conjecture is also difficult, however, since Kavod also needs students actually did love each other and were very committed to the words of their teacher "to love one another" yet, it was precisely because of their love that they felt the need to impress their ideas upon their fellow students.* Imagine you have just discovered a great secret to happiness, and you are so convinced that this information can heal the world, would you not want to impart this secret to all the people you love? Would you perhaps want to scream it from the rooftops? If you were so convinced, would you not be insistent, or even a bit aggressive in your mission? Would you not be as the sign of the month, the *Shor* / the bull or Taurus, and adamantly express yourself and your opinions? If you were not assertive, perhaps it would seem that you lacked love for others and did not care for their well-being.

The problem, of course, is that just like you have your insights, so do others. Because of your 'love' for others you wish to change their way of thinking, but when they are resistant you become aggressive. Your proselytizing, which to you feels like an expression of love and concern, may thus be perceived by some as judgmental,

---

to be given to one's students, as Rabbi Eliezer (who was a student of Rabbi Akiva, *Zevachim*, 93a) teaches, "Let the *Kavod* of your student be as dear to you as your own" (*Avos*, 4:12). On the other hand, perhaps Rabbi Eliezer taught this in reaction to the lack of Kavod that he observed among the 24,000 students of Rabbi Akiva.

* Although, it does seem from other sources that they did not 'care' about each other on some level, as they did not visit each other when sick (See *Nedarim* 40a). We also find that they did not respect the other great sages of the time (*Menachos* 68b). The reverse could therefore also be argued: because his students did not respect each other, because they did not love each other, and because the consequence of this was death, therefore Rabbi Akiva came to believe that "loving your fellow is the great principle of Torah." In other words, perhaps he came to this realization *after* the events with his students. Although, see *Likutei Sichos*, 32, p.149, note 7.

condescending, or worse even. In such an instance, your advances are most likely to come across as disrespecting their ways of thinking and life choices. Ultimately, it will become clear that your good intentions are tangled in arrogance.

Interestingly, the first time strife is recorded in the Torah, is when Hashem tells the Snake, "And I will put enmity between you and the woman" (*Bereishis*, 3:15). The Hebrew word for enmity is v'Eiva. According to the Zohar (*Zohar* 3, 79a), this word is numerically twenty-four. And indeed, this word, this concept of enmity is the meta-root of the death of the twenty-four (thousand) students of Rabbi Akiva, who passed from this world because they did not have respect and were not amicable towards each other. At, first when Chavah was created, the Torah says *"Va'Ya'Vieha /* and he brought her, to the man." The word V'aYa'Vieha is also numerically twenty-four, as the Zohar teaches (*Zohar* 1, 48b). So, they started with love and connection, but then, through various breakdowns of communication and a desire to share the fruits of a new perspective with the other, they descended into strife. It is the same with the students of Rabbi Akiva, they loved each other so much, that it brought them to a place of not respecting each other, and perhaps worse.

A slightly different way of viewing this episode with the students of Rabbi Akiva is that they *did* love each other, but their love was not balanced with *Kavod*. The word *Kavod* is normally translated as 'honor,' yet *Kavod* is related to, and spelled the same, as the word *Kaved /* heavy (see *Targum Unkulus*, Shemos, 17:12, where the Targum translates the word, "heavy" as, "honor"). According to this perspective, *Kavod* means to subscribe to the other person a degree of importance, weight, and honor. Certainly, it is possible to love someone (as a member of your group) without ascribing to them any individual importance.

Kavod is a basic human necessity. The *Nefesh* / animating soul of the human being is called *Kavod* (*Ba'al HaMaor*, in the beginning of Berachos. see also *Pirush Rabbeinu Yonah*, Mishlei, 1:22), as we see in the following verses: "That my *Kavod* / soul may sing your praises and not be silent" (*Tehilim*, 30:12), and, "*Ura K'vodi* / Awaken, my soul" (*Tehilim*, 57:9). A basic psychological need of human beings is to sense that they are respected and taken seriously, that their life has 'weight.'

It is all too easy to 'love' another, and even give them financial or emotional support, while still remaining subtly aloof or even 'superior' and patronizing. For example, with a feeling of love we may send charity to help the less fortunate, but do we really regard the recipients as personally important and honorable in and of themselves? One litmus test is, are we as comfortable receiving from others as we are giving? If not, perhaps we are giving charity from a position 'above' the receivers, and avoiding their actual *Kavod* and weightiness. Perhaps in the act of giving charity, we are really potentially *receiving* something, and from a very important person at that.

Similarly, can we listen to what others have to say, or do we prefer to do all the talking? People who are driven to insert their opinions into every conversation may be suffering from a 'superiority complex.' Such self-absorption was the downfall of the students of Rabbi Akiva. They believed in "love your neighbor like yourself," and they loved and supported their colleagues, but they kept their *Kavod* for themselves. They did not open themselves to hear their fellow students' different ways of thinking and understanding (The Rashbi was the opposite. He gave Kavod to the words of his colleagues. *Yerushalmi, Shevi'is,* 9:1. *Tosefos, Pesachim,* 51b, Ani). Their love was ultimately self-centered and self-serving.

Indeed, the whole idea of Kavod is intrinsically connected with intellectual respect, as Kavod itself is associated with intellect, as Rabbeinu Yonah (Spain, 1200- 1263), the great moralist and *Tzadik*, writes (*Pirush Rabbeinu Yonah*, Mishlei, 1:22). In the poignant words of the Rambam, "One who is not careful with the honor of his Creator" means, someone that is not careful with their intellect. This is because *Siechel* / the power to think is considered to be the *Kavod Hashem* / the honor of Hashem (*Pirush Ha'Mishnayos*, Chagigah 2:1). In the context of our story, each of the students may have had Kavod for themselves, and revealed Kavod Hashem by using their intellect to decipher and deeply understand their Rebbe's teachings, and perhaps they even truly loved each other, but, they lacked *Kavod* for each other, and as a result they did not give weight to their colleagues' opinions.

Regarding their teacher, the Mishnah says, "When Rabbi Akiva Passed away the Kavod of Torah was lost" (*Mishnah Sotah*, 49a). Rashi (*ad loc*) writes that Rabbi Akiva explicated and explained every *Kotz* / tiny detail of the forms of the letters of the Torah, and this was an example of *Kavod haTorah*. In other words, Rabbi Akiva gave the Torah so much Kavod, he ascribed so much weight to its every mark and utterance, that he did not just seek to interpret the meanings of the words, but he sought to understand the deeper significance of the letters themselves, down to their smallest dot and point. Kavod can thus mean giving weight, meaning, or importance to every single detail that a person is telling you. When you do this, you are open not only to *what* the person is telling you, but *how* they are saying it, the words they choose, their gestures, emotions, character traits, and subtler cues as well as surrounding energies. From this perspective: everything has meaning, nothing is superfluous. This is real Kavod.

Giving Kavod to others does not come so easily. Among the 24,000 students, there were many who were friends when they were growing up. That situation can sometimes present the hardest challenge in fostering a sense of honor and weight between friends. A person may think, 'that childhood friend of mine who used to disrupt class and play hooky is now supposedly a mature, noble Torah sage or accomplished professional?' It is precisely this inability of friends to take each other seriously that sheds more light into the death of the students of Rabbi Akiva.

Real *Kavod* means to honor and respect every beautiful aspect of the other person, to *Doresh* / search out and delve into the nuances of every person we meet. To take every detail of their personality 'seriously.' Certainly, not to judge or evaluate them for who they were yesterday, or as children.

The famed Chassidic Rebbe, known as the Maggid of Kozhnitz, writes (*Avodas Yisrael*) on the following verse, "*Tzama Nafshi l'Elohim, l'E-l Chai, Masai Avo v'Eira'eh P'nei Elo-him* / My soul thirsts for Elokim, for the Living G-d, when will I come and see the face of Elokim" (*Tehilim* 63:2). Says the Maggid, "My soul yearns ...*l'E-l Chai* / to the living G-d," the words *E-l* (31) *Chai* (18) are together numerically 49. This means, we desire and yearn for You during these 49 days between Pesach and Shavuos. We yearn for Matan Torah, we yearn for *Gadlus* / expansive awareness, we yearn to get out of our *Tuma* / stuckness, we yearn for Unity.

E-l Chai means Living G-d. We want to have a relationship with the Master of the universe that is alive and present from moment-to-moment. If our relationship with Hashem has not grown today, has not deepened, and it is the same as yesterday, than we are in a relationship with a 'molten god,' Heaven forbid. "Do not make yourselves gods out of cast metal" (*Vayikra*, 19:4). Writes the Mei haShiloach (Kedoshim): this means, do not have a stale relationship with the Creator of the world. Do not make your relationship with Hashem, with the *E-l Chai*, as a cast, fixed, frozen and stuck in the past. Our relationship with Hashem should always be fluid, open, conscious, and dynamic. Our relationship is dead if it is not happening in the present. This is what we truly yearn for during the days of *Sefiras haOmer*, during this time of *Katnus* / diminished consciousness and separation.

If this is true in relationship to the Creator of the universe, it is also true interpersonally. But why was there such a harsh consequence for an interpersonal problem? The answer is that the way we view others affects them. Perhaps the 24,000 students were 'dying' in this period because they saw each other in a fixed or 'dead' way. In other words, the students were not able to see each other as being in process, as who they had become or were becoming, but only as who they were. In any case, cultivating 'living' relationships is something we need to work on during the Omer period. We need to ensure that we have *Kavod* for others, not merely aloof or self-aggrandizing 'love.' We should practice being open from moment to moment, recognizing that others are just as fluid, evolving, and alive as we are. We can honor their aliveness when we are non-judgmentally present with the way they are in each unique moment.

In another related story from roughly the same time period, the Gemara teaches that the Second Temple was destroyed for an overabundance of *Sinas Chinam* / baseless hatred between the Sages. Thinking about this in terms of Rabbi Akiva's students and *Sefiras haOmer*, we can see that the month of Iyyar is an opportune time to grow in the practice of *Ahavas Chinam* / 'unconditional, selfless love.' Not by chance, the numerical value of the words *Ahavas Chinam* is 506, the same value as the sign of the month, *Shor* / bull or Taurus. Our aggressive 'bull' nature should be yoked into true selfless love and Kavod. When we make this Tikkun during this month, we will have made it easier for ourselves to give respect and honor to others throughout the year.

Based on all of the previous considerations, the time between Pesach and Shavuos can therefore be seen more as a period of introspection and self-evaluation, as opposed to strict mourning. This need for self-evaluation, often connected to the deaths of Rabbi Akiva's students, as explored above, originally has to do with the lowly state of the Nation of Israel after coming out of Egypt, "They (the Egyptians) were idol worshipers and they (the Nation of Israel) were also idol worshipers" (*Medrash*). It is taught that the Israelites had fallen to the forty-ninth level of impurity while living in Egypt. Thus, the forty-nine days of *Sefiras haOmer* can be seen to counterbalance each one of those levels, returning us to a state of integral alignment in order that we may receive the Torah on the fiftieth day after leaving Egypt. Also, on a more personal level, after the initial excitement of the arrival of spring, we all have a natural need to turn towards introspection and self-evaluation. As the warming weather pulls us out into the world, it is wise to find our center first so we are not completely thrown off balance by all the new energy abounding.

In the month of Elul, there is also a concept of self-evaluation, yet it is a self-evaluation that is generally in relationship to ourselves. In Iyyar, our self-evaluation is primarily focused on our relationships and interactions with others.. This is because in Elul we are preparing to enter the winter months which are naturally more solitary. In Iyyar we are preparing to enter the summer months when we are naturally more outgoing. Also, in Iyyar we recently came out of the lonely winter months. Now that we will be engaging more with others we need to evaluate ourselves to ensure that our interpersonal relationships are in order.

A Maturing Process

Nisan, the month of the birth of our people, represents a state of pre-individuation, as we are spiritually like an infant, having just been born through the Exodus. Iyyar corresponds to a process of individuation, wandering through the desert, finding our way. We do not cut our hair, and are for a time a little bit like a wild, untamed child. Sivan corresponds to trans-individuation, maturity, and a general openness to others, as we approach the mountain of revelation and receptivity.

In Iyyar we develop our self-expression. In this phase of the maturing process comes the emergence of personality; we can easily err into self-involvement and not respecting the needs of others. We have a custom of studying *Pirkei Avos* / Ethics of our Fathers during this period, because we need to harness our self-expression to holiness. The month of Iyyar is therefore a time to create a healthy balance and boundaries between self and other. This is a necessary stage before receiving the Torah, which is an acceptance of ultimate concern and responsibility. This is also why we work hard to refine and illuminate our actions during this month through the Counting of the Omer.

Nisan is the astrological sign of a meek lamb. In this developmental stage there is no me or you, — there is not yet a perception of individual selves. A newborn infant looks almost the same as any other, and he/she is not yet actively expressing personality, let alone pushing its own agenda. This is a pre-personal stage. There is no real 'me' as of yet.

Later, the child starts to discover himself and express his individuality. The bull of Iyyar is not characterized by meek submission, but rather strong confidence and self-assertion. In this stage there is a strong 'me' but not a real 'you.' At times there are instances of selfishness and insensitivity — a child of two (or even twelve) does not usually want to share. This is the developmental stage of personality.

Finally the child matures enough to begin responsibly acknowledging others. He must now co-exist and share with other people. This point of maturity is reached in Sivan, the month of Gemini /

twins, representing a consciousness of both 'me' and 'you.' This is a trans-personal stage.

Nisan is pre-individuation, life as a young infant. Iyyar is individuation, life as a wild, untamed and expressive child. Sivan is trans-individuation, maturity, and an acute sense of responsibility. .

The *Sefirah* period is paradoxically about asserting self while at the same time working to more deeply acknowledge and respect others. That is the essential balancing act of Iyyar. This is one reason we do not cut our hair during this period. Hair is a form of self-expression. We have to experience this developmental stage before we can move on to maturity. On Lag b'Omer we are allowed to cut our hair, as it is time to rein in the wildness of our self-expression, and achieve the *Tikkun* for not having properly respected others.

This process mirrors the month's permutation of the Divine Name, as discussed above (Yud-Hei-Hei-Vav). Yud and Hei, the first two letters of the Name, are in their intended order, and thus channel the energy of *Chesed*. This is reflected in the people's uncut, flowing hair during the first half of the month. The final two letters, Hei-Vav, are in reverse order, and thus channel *Din*. This corresponds to the cutting and crafting of the hair mid-way through the month, as raw energies begin to be brought into balance. The message of Iyyar is that both sides of this existential coin are necessary. We need space for the self to be free, and we need time for our soul to be good.

Related to this dichotomy of self-expression and soul-development we learn that King *Shlomo* / Solomon started building the Beis HaMikdash, "on the second day, of the second month" (*Divrei*

Hayamim 1, 3:1). Additionally, it is taught that the wise and mighty King Shlomo received help to build the Beis HaMikdash from humans as well as from *Sheidim* / spirits (*Medrash Rabbah,* Shemos, 54: 4). Ontologically, *Sheidim* fall somewhere in between the natural and angelic worlds. Meaning that they do not necessarily function according to the laws of any one realm of reality. They are thus somewhat unpredictable and also energetically powerful in relation to humans, making them risky to employ or interact with. We learn in the Talmud that King Shlomo had numerous dealings with these 'incomplete angles' (*Gitin,* 68a-b), but in the end he was triumphant over them (i.e. they never got the best of him) (*Sanhedrin,* 20b). From this perspective, we can now more deeply understand the significance of bringing a *Se'or* / barley offering, which was considered more of an animal feed than a food for humans (*Sotah,* 14a), in the month of Iyyar during the Omer period. *Se'or* has the same root letters as the word *Se'ir* / hair, which is itself related to the concept of *Sheidim* (*Rashi,* Vayikra, 17: 7. *Torahs Kohanim,* 17:100). It was therefore specifically during Iyyar — when on the one hand we do not cut our hair, representing the free expression of our more wild/raw energies; while at the same time we are counting the Omer, representing our disciplined commitment to self-reflection and refinement — that King Shlomo was able to harness and channel both his and the *Sheidim's* raw energy into building the holy Beis HaMikdash.

As mentioned, when Klal Yisrael left Egypt in the month of Nisan, they did not receive the Torah until the month of Sivan. During the month of Iyyar they were already freed from the bondage of Egypt, but had not yet assumed the responsibility of Torah; they were in a way, *Hefker* / ownerless. They were *Hefker,* as they had just escaped slavery and had not yet accepted the Torah, and they were also in a place of Hefker, as they were traveling through a vast expanse of empty desert (*Medrash Rabbah,* Bamidbar, 1:7).

Following Nisan, they journeyed from a per-individuation state, as a child who is just born, into Iyyar, where there is a strong sense of toddler-like or adolescent individuality. During this time they explored and expressed their wilderness energy, while at the same time they kept gradually working on themselves until they reached the mature state of Sivan — ready, willing, and able to receive the Torah, which is an acceptance of ultimate concern and responsibility in relationship to both Creator and creation.*

Throughout the Omer period, and especially during the month of Iyyar, we are moving from the *Omer* / barley offering (animal food) to the *Shtei Lechem* / two Bread Loaves (human food) that we offer on Shavuos. This means that during the time of Sefirah we are working on elevating our consciousness from the level of an

---

* To extend the metaphor of pregnancy and birth connected to the going out of Egypt, we can think of the next stage in our development following the birth of the Exodus as *Yenikah* / suckling. (The two Israelites who prophesied in the desert had names related to Yenikah — *El-Dad* / to the bosom, and *M'dad* / from the bosom (*Mishnas Chassidim,* haChalav, 1:1). During the 40 years in the desert we were as a suckling (*Devarim,* 32:13) in need of our Mother's milk. After traveling in the desert for some 30 days, the Manna descended in Iyyar. The Manna was a white seed, reminiscent of milk (*Shemos,* 16:31). Much like mother's milk, the Manna contained all tastes imaginable (*Yumah* 75a). Moshe was, in some way, like a mother who carried and gave birth to Klal Yisrael, "Was I pregnant with this entire people; did I give birth to them?" (*Bamidbar,* 11:12). The Ohr HaChayim (ad loc) reads this quote not as a question but rather as a statement. Moshe is saying that in the Desert he was the mother of Klal Yisrael. Indeed, our sages tell us that the Manna descended "in the merit" of Moshe (*Ta'anis,* 9a). Ultimately, we reached final *Mochin* / mind and maturity after the 40 years in the Desert (*Devarim,* 29:3. *Avodah Zarah,* 5b). Then we were ready to enter into the Holy Land to make a 'permanent home' with Hashem.

animal (a traditional image of selfishness and insensitivity) to the more transcendental level of an honorable human being.

"Who is honorable? One who honors others" (*Pirkei Avos*, 4:1). This is the inner work and Tikkun of this period between Pesach and Shavuos, with Iyyar being the bulk of the time. From the careful counting of each day and the compassionate consideration of our soul from forty-nine different angles, to studying *Pirkei Avos* and refraining from cutting our hair for the first half of the month — Iyyar is a portal of time in which we move from the state of a meek lamb (infancy/Nisan), enter into the energy of a strong bull (youth/Iyyar), and prepare for the revelation of real relationship (maturity/Sivan).

SUMMARY OF IYYAR

12 DIMENSIONS OF IYYAR	
Sequence of Hashem's Name	Yud-Hei Hei-Vav (half of the name is the correct sequence/*Rachamim* and half is a reversed sequence/*Din*)
Torah Verse	*Yis-halel...Ha-mis-halel Ha-maskil V'yade'a* / Let he that glories glory in this: that he understands and knows (Me) (Yirmiyahu, 9:23)
Letter	Vav (ו)
Month Name	*Iyyar* / bright
Sense	*Hirhur* / Subtle Thought
Zodiac	*Shor* / the bull or Taurus
Tribe	*Yisachar* / Issachar
Body Part	Right Kidney
Element	*Afar* / Earth
Parshios	*Tazria-Metzorah* through *Bechukosai* (each Parsha dealing with Din, Tumah or the rhythms of time)
Season	Second Month of Spring
Holiday	Lag b'Omer

SUMMARY

In this **time of year,** the second month of Spring, our individuality begins to assert itself more, even like an aggressive bull (the **astrological sign** of the month). Therefore, we need to balance our personal attributes by humbly bringing *Binah* / understanding into them, as alluded to in the **verse** of the month: *Yis-halel... Ha-mis-halel Ha-maskil V'yade'a* / Let he that glories, glory in this: that he understands and knows (Me) (Yirmiyahu 9:23). In addition to 'knowing Hashem,' this verse also alludes to 'knowing oneself.' This is accomplished by consciously reflecting on and inter-connecting our attributes, alluded to by the **letter** of connection, Vav. For example (as alluded to by this month's **sequence of Hashem's name**), we need to connect our *Chesed* / kindness or expansiveness, with our *Din* / strictness or contractiveness. We do this work of self-refinement throughout most of this month without any external inspiration, like the cold, dry **element** of earth.

When we have thus accomplished certain levels of refinement, we can begin to receive Divine 'advice,' which is transmitted to us through the **body part** of Iyyar, our right kidney. The subtle intelligence we cultivate in this way is called *Hirhur*, the **'sense'** of the month. *Hirhur* includes a sensitive understanding of the cycles of time, known to be a defining characteristic of the **tribe** of the month, Yisachar.

We must also develop a longing for our Creator during this month, and a yearning for the revelation of Torah, like a lover who has been separated from their beloved. When the **holiday** of Lag b'Omer arrives, this yearning releases a powerful *Ziv* / brightness (the original **name of the month**), with the revelation of the hidden Torah, the *Zohar* / Illumination of Rabbi Shimon bar Yochai.

It is to this revelation, and to the story of *Rashbi* / Rabbi Shimon bar Yochai, that we will shortly turn our attention.

PRACTICE
Counting the Omer

The primary practice of Iyyar is the Counting of the Omer. As discussed previously, Iyyar is the only month completely dedicated to Counting the Omer, making this the defining spiritual feature of its time, being as it is empty of any Torah-based or Rabbinic holidays. Each day we count another day, and each day we focus on another corresponding attribute or *Sefirah*. Every day we fix another interpersonal issue, and remember that the count up from one to forty-nine is actually a count-down, from *Chesed* to *Malchus*, an expression of our longing for the arrival of Matan Torah.

During each of the seven weeks of the Omer we work on one of seven basic character traits. The first attribute of each pair is the supporting or motivational attribute, and the second is the actual emotion that we're working on throughout that week. For example, on day one of the counting, we think about "Chesed of Chesed." We ask ourselves, 'Is my kindness really motivated by kindness? When I give, is it out of kindness, or are there ulterior motives and side-benefits at play?' On the second day, we think about "Gevurah of Chesed." 'Is my kindness supported by discipline? Am I giving with appropriate balance, and to the right recipients?' Every day there is another aspect of consciousness and action to check and evaluate.

WEEK 1: *Chesed* / kindness or giving. During this week we are working on our giving nature: Are we giving enough? Is our giving balanced?

WEEK 2: *Gevurah* / strength or restriction. During this week we are working on our discipline: Do we have enough discipline to accomplish what we are called to accomplish? Is our discipline applied to the most appropriate areas of our life?

WEEK 3: *Tiferes* / beauty or harmony. During this week we are working on achieving harmony: Is our life harmonious? Are we well-adjusted and balanced? Are we in harmony with others?

WEEK 4: *Netzach* / victory or perseverance. During this week we are working on our perseverance: Are we persevering with our ambitions and following through with our resolutions? Is our perseverance balanced with the other attributes, for example, humility?

WEEK 5: *Hod* / splendor or humility. During this week we are working on our humility: Do we have enough healthy humility in our lives? Is our humility holding us back or is it properly balanced with confidence?

WEEK 6: *Yesod* / foundation or alignment. During this week we are working on our alignment: Do we have focus in our lives? Are all aspects of ourselves — our mind, heart, and body — aligned?

WEEK 7: *Malchus* / kingship (dignity) or receptivity. During this week we are working on our receptivity: Do we know how to receive? Do we do so with dignity? Is our desire to receive from another opening us up to more — physically, mentally, emotionally, and spiritually — or is it closing us off from our own self-generated proactive potential?

The word *Sefirah* is related to the word *Sapir* / shine. As we are counting each day of the Omer, and refining our character traits, we begin to shine with Divine attributes. We are thus building the inner vessels to be able to receive, with the arrival of Matan Torah, the brilliant light of *Mochin d'Gadlus* / expansive consciousness and total clarity.*

---

* The *Mochin* / clarity that we receive on the night of Pesach is a miraculous gift from above, and is thus fleeting. The next day, in order to build proper vessels to draw down *Mochin* / intellect into our *Middos* / emotions and attributes, we begin counting the Sefirah (Rashash, *Nahar Shalom*, p. 64). More specifically, through *Sefiras haOmer* we are building the *Middos* or vessels of *Tiferes* and *Malchus*, which were previously in a state of *Gadlus* / maturity and filled with *Mochin* / mind on Pesach Night. After Pesach, these vessels experience a corresponding *Katnus* / diminishment and through our counting and inner work during the seven weeks of the Omer, we rebuild these vessels in a sustainable, stronger, and even more sensitive way (*Sha'ar HaKavanos*, *Derush* 3, Pesach). During week one, the Chochmah of Tiferes is perfected. In week two, it is the Binah of Tiferes; in week three, the Chesed of Da'as of Tiferes; in week four, the Gevurah of Da'as of Tiferes; in week five, the Chesed of Tiferes; in week six, the Gevurah of Tiferes. In week seven, the Tiferes of Tiferes is perfected, and with it Malchus (*Sha'ar HaKavanos*, Chag haShavuos).

During the month of Iyyar we experience both *Tohu* / chaos, freedom and wilderness, and the ability of *Tikkun* / fixing, attunement, balance, and order. Counting the Omer during this time enables us to be fully present in each step of the journey, from slavery to Sinai. This identification, unification, and elevation of our soul in time empowers us to channel the *Light of Tohu* into the *Vessels of Tikkun*.

Having explored the first eleven themes and categories in relation to the month of Iyyar, we will now delve into an extended discussion about the nature of *Lag b'Omer*, the 33rd day of the Omer, the 18th of Iyyar.

PART TWO:

Lag B'Omer
THE 33RD DAY OF THE OMER
A Day of Celebration within a Season of Mourning

The period of counting the Omer is generally understood as a time of Din, mourning, and introspection. Why is it so? And why is the 18th of Iyyar, the 33rd day of the Omer, a day of celebration?

As we have already mentioned, our sages tell us that the 24,000 students of Rabbi Akiva died during the period between Pesach and Shavuos. The consensus of the *Poskim* / codifiers of Torah law is that within these 49 days the students actually only died on 34 of those days (*Bach, Orach Chayim,* Siman 493). There are various opinions on how these 34 days are distributed throughout the 49. According to all opinions, however, the month of Iyyar is a time of Din and mourning, and this is apparently related to the death of Rabbi Akiva's 24,000 students.

The Gemara / Talmud itself does not mention that the mourning period was established specifically because of the death of the students of Rabbi Akiva, it only records the sad narrative of their deaths. The establishment of a formal mourning period seems to have occurred much later, during the early Middle Ages, or perhaps in the times of the Gemara but only publicly discussed in the times of the Geonim (589 CE - 1038). The first mention of the prohibition against getting married during this period is from the time of the Geonim.

Rav Natroi Gaon writes, "Regarding your question of why we do not betroth or marry in the period between Pesach and Shavuos ... (it is) a custom of mourning...the 12,000 pairs of students that died between Pesach and Shavuos... Earlier generations were (also) accustomed during these days not to marry...." Regarding the prohibition against cutting hair during this period, Rav Aharon Hakohen of Lunil (early 14th Century) writes in *Orachos Chayim*, "The custom is not to marry from Pesach until Shavuos and we also do not cut our hair, out of mourning for the 12,000 pairs of students..." The *Shulchan Aruch* / Code of Jewish Law writes that we do not marry or take haircuts or dance during this period.[*]

---

[*] The laws of mourning, such as refraining from playing live music, cutting hair, and getting married during the days of Sefirah, are not mentioned in the Gemara, nor in the Rambam. Yet, the Tur (*Orach Chayim*, 493) writes, "All people have the custom to not marry nor cut their hair during these days." The notion of not marrying during these days dates back at least to the time of the Geonim. Hair cutting is first mentioned in the Rishonim. Music playing or dancing, seems to be a much later custom.

While the Omer period is a time of partial mourning, it is not necessarily a 'sad' time,* rather it is a time of self inspection and longing to connect with our souls as well as with Hashem, as will be explored. Yet this is still a valid question: why, amid an extended time of mourning, is there a mini-holiday called Lag b'Omer? What is the reason for this day of celebration? There are various ways to understand this.

Opinion One: The first time we find Lag b'Omer being identified as a festive day is in the Rishonim. They note that we are not allowed to fast on this day, since there is a tradition that the students of Rabbi Akiva ceased dying. As the Meiri (*Yevamos*, 62b) brings down in the name of the Geonim, "They stopped dying on the 33rd of Omer" (*Shulchan Aruch haRav*, 493:5), and this is the reason to celebrate.**

---

* One example of this not being a 'sad' time is that this period is also called *Chol haMoed* (*Ramban*, Vayikra, 23:16), meaning the intermediate festival days between the holiday of Pesach and with Shavuos. The laws of Chol haMoed ask us to refrain from marrying and getting haircuts for reasons unrelated to mourning.

** The Mechaber, Rabbi Yoseph Caro, writes however in *Orach Chayim*, Siman 493 that they died from the second day of Pesach until (after) the 34rd day. The last day they died was on the 34th and they stopped dying on the 35th day forward. So mourning is for the first 34 days of the Omer, afterward we can cut our hair, make weddings, etc. Yet, being that *Miktzas haYom keKulo* / part of the day is like the whole day (see *Aruch Hashulchan*, 493:4), a person can thus take a haircut and can marry, from the morning of the 34th day of the Omer. The Rishon, Rabbi Yehoshua Ibn Shuaiv (1280 - ca 1340), a student of the Rashba, writes, that he 'heard' that the students of Rabbi Akiva stopped dying on the 34th of the Omer, and thus, from the 34th day of the Omer people take haircuts (*Derasha L'Pesach*, Yom Rishon). The argument that, "They stopped dying on the 34th" is also the opinion of the Tashbetz, Rabbi Shimon ben Tzemach Duran (1361-1444) (*Magen Avos*, 1:1), (Chidah, *Maaris Ayin*, Yevamos, 62b), as well as the opinion of Mechaber.

Interestingly, the word *Avel* / mourner is numerically 33, an allusion to the death of the students of Rabbi Akiva on the first 33 days of the Omer (Rabbi Moshe Dovid Valle, *Sefer HaLikutim* 2, p. 552).

According to this opinion, there is nothing about Lag b'Omer per se to celebrate, rather "from" Lag b'Omer forward (or Lad/34th of the Omer) the students stopped dying, and thus this day is marked. In this way, Lag b'Omer is not really a joyous day to celebrate, as all the students died (besides five) and there was no one else left to die. Rather, since we no longer mourn their passing, there is a "little joy" (in the words of the Alter Rebbe, *ibid*) as life resumes to normal*.

The Maharal, Rabbi Yehudah Loew of Prague (1525-1609), points out that the numerical value of the word *Kavod* / honor (referring to the honor that the students did not show towards each other) is 32 (see also, *Sefer HaBahir*, 134). This alludes to the view that they only died on the first 32 days of the Omer and ceased dying on the 33rd day.**

* It is also possible that Lag b'Omer is singled out for celebration, since according to the *Ramban* (Vayikra, 23:16), the time period between Pesach and Shavuos is *Chol haMoed* / intermediate semi-festival days. On *Chol haMoed* it is a Mitzvah to be joyful. When the students of Rabbi Akiva were dying, the nationwide response of mourning pushed aside the joy of Chol haMoed, but once they stopped dying, the joy returned.

** Regarding *Kavod:* when people do not respect each other, they are not humble enough to receive and acknowledge even healthy constructive criticism. The following is a *Remez* / allusion to the connection between constructive criticism, Lag b'Omer, and being respectful.

There are 50 gates of understanding (*Rosh Hashanah*, 21b. *Nedarim*, 38a). In his lifetime Moshe attained only the 49th level of understanding (*ibid*), and thus he was unable to cross the Jordan River (whose width was 50 cubits (*Tosafos*, *Sotah*, 34b)) and enter the Holy Land (see also *Devarim*, 3:25, *Ba'al HaTurim*). Only at the moment of his death, when he had ascended Mount Nevo, did he attain the 50th level. The words *Mount Nevo*, which can be read 'the Mount which has *Nun* (50) / 'the 50th gate' *Bo* / in it.

Being as it is a day of humility and acceptance of criticism, on Lag b'Omer there is an extra measure of the *Koach* / energy of *Kavod* / honor. Because this day gives strength to be respectful and humble, on this day the students of Rabbi Akiva did not die.

Opinion Two: On Lag b'Omer something extraordinary occurred. Rabbi Moshe Isserles (1520-1572), the Rema, writes that miraculously none of the students died on the 33rd day of the Omer, although they did continue to die from after Lag b'Omer until a few days before Shavuos. This is the reason we celebrate on the 33rd, as something extraordinary occurred on that day. It is worth pointing out that the Rema's own *Yahrtzeit* / day of passing is on Lag b'Omer.

Opinion Three: The simple language of the Gemara (*Yevamos*, 62b) says, "They died between Pesach and *Atzeres* (Shavuos)," meaning across the span of all 49 days. However, it also suggests that within this period of 49 days they only died on regular weekdays; they did not die on Shabbos, the Festival days of Pesach, or on Rosh Chodesh. There is a total of seven Shabbosim in 49 days, and they did not die on the 7 days of Yom Tov (Pesach), and the 3 days of Rosh

---

If Moshe, the embodiment of Torah wisdom, attained the level of 49, we can assume that other prophets can attain, at the very best, only the 48th level. Indeed, the prophets only attained the 48th level, alluded to in the verse "Many women have acquired חיל / wealth..."*Mishlei*, 31:29); the word חיל is numerically 48 (Gra, *Kol Eliyahu HaShaleim*, Nifloas Eliyahu, p.11). A prophet is the individual embodiment of the spiritual quality of the people, and a leader resembles the people. We are therefore *collectively* on the 48th level. Corresponding to this, there are 48 major (male) prophets of old (*Megilah*, 14a). The Mishnah in *Avos* (6:6) elaborates on 48 qualities through which the Torah is acquired. The 33rd quality that the Mishnah mentions is, "One who appreciates (constructive) criticism." A truly humble person can accept criticism. Indeed, the Sefirah connected to Lag b'Omer is Hod of Hod, indicating deep humility and also *l'Hodos* / to respectfully acknowledge another. Thus, insofar as they were respectful on the 33rd day, they miraculously did not die on that day.

Chodesh. The sum of these days is 7+7+3= 17. Subtract 17 from 49 days, and there are 32 days of dying. They did not die on the holy days, those which are informally called *Yamim Tovim* / good days; the word *Tov* is also numerically 17.

This opinion is that of Rabbi Ya'akov Moelin, known as the Maharil (c.1365-1427) (*Sefer haMinhagim*, 749). He continues, "as we know the students died for 32 days in total, therefore we celebrate on the 33rd day, as a *symbolic* time of their ceasing to die." In actuality, they *did* die on the day of Lag b'Omer, as it is one of the normal weekdays between Pesach and Shavuos.

Opinion Four: Rabbi Shmuel Eidels (1555-1631), known as the Maharsha, gives another reason that we celebrate Lag b'Omer in connection with the death of the students of Rabbi Akiva (Maharsha, *Moed Katan*, 28a). Once the 32 days have past, the *Rov* / majority of the Omer has past, and therefore on the 33rd day of Sefirah it is a time to celebrate. To clarify this point: the 49 days of Sefirah divided by three equal 16 ⅓ days. While a strict majority would be 51 percent, a 'supermajority' is two thirds, or in this case 32 ⅔ days. Thus, when we pass this mark and enter the remaining 17 days (*Tov* / good = 17) there is a return to joy.

These are four basic reasons explaining why the celebration on Lag b'Omer is connected to the 24,000 students of Rabbi Akiva. The 33rd day of the Omer is 1) the day they stopped dying, or the last day that they died, 2) the day they miraculously did not die, even though they continued to die throughout the rest of the Omer, 3) a symbolic day, representing the ceasing of the students' deaths after 32 ⅔ days or 4) the passing of the supermajority of the Sefirah period.

The Day of Rashbi

In addition to the death of the 24,000 students of Rabbi Akiva, there is another well-known reason for the celebration of the 33rd day of the Omer. Years after these terrible deaths, one of Rabbi Akiva's five surviving students, *Rashbi* / Rabbi Shimon Bar Yochai, passed away on the 33rd day of the Omer.* Lag b'Omer is thus also universally associated with celebrating the life and death of Rashbi. For one thing, Rashbi died a natural death, unlike the other students. The 24,000 students died young in a time period which is usually connected to healing, as mentioned earlier. This fact forces us to view their deaths as a kind of aberration, or supernatural event (*Maharsha*, Yevamos, 62b). Rashbi, however, lived to a ripe old age and died a natural death. Rashbi's idyllic death, with his closest students gathered around him in spiritual rapture on the 33rd day of the Omer, thus signals a fixing for the death of the 24,000 students, and a return to *Seder* / order and *Shefa* / flow in the world.

Lag b'Omer falls on the 18th day of Iyyar. The number 18 in Hebrew is spelled Yud/10, Ches/8. These letters spell *Chai* / life. *Chai Iyyar* is thus the 'Life of Iyyar,' the day that life triumphs over death. The numerical value of the word *Iyyar* is 221 (Aleph/1, Yud/10, Yud/10, Reish/200), which is the same as the word *Erech*

---

* This day has been confirmed as the day of his passing by spiritual luminaries such as the Alter Rebbe, the *Yaros Devash* (2:11), the *Bnei Yissaschar*, the *Aruch haShulchan*, and all the great sages of the past 300 years. See also *Birchei Yoseph* (Chidah, Siman 493). Lag b'Omer is a time that *Klal Yisrael* / the prophetic super-conscious collective of Israel, established to celebrate and commemorate the passing of Rashbi.

/ lengthened. In this way, the phrase *Chai Iyyar* alludes to *Erech Chai* / length of life (Maharal, *Nesivos Olam*, Nesiv Torah, 12). The *Ko'ach* / power of Lag b'Omer is to renew, lengthen, enhance, and perpetuate life.

Seen from this perspective, Lag b'Omer is a celebration of Rashbi's full and fruitful life as well as his natural death. In this sense, Lag b'Omer reveals that we do not need a supernatural event in order to establish a sacred celebration, all we need is to focus on a fruitful life and a natural death. We do not need a miracle from Above to justify singing and dancing for joy. One theme of Lag b'Omer is thus to *reveal* the latent Divine joy within normative, mundane experience. In fact, the word *Lag* read backward is *Gal* / reveal.

Additionally, Rashbi actually requested that we celebrate his day of passing (*Idra Zuta*, Zohar 3, 291a. *Mishnas Chassidim*, Maseches Iyyar v'Sivan. *See also Pri Chadash, Orach Chayim*, 493). Therefore, one essential reason why Lag b'Omer is a celebratory holiday, is simply that Rashbi instructed his students to celebrate, rather than mourn, the day of his passing.

Iyyar is a month that is empty of the life-giving presence of Torah-based holidays. Lag b'Omer, however, comes to us on the 18th day of Iyyar. As mentioned, the number 18 is a numerological symbol of *Chai* / life. The 18th of Iyyar is the *Chayus* / aliveness of Iyyar. It is a day to celebrate life, and it is a day that revivifies us. Rashbi dies, as the Zohar in the Idra Zuta tells us, while reciting this verse, "…There Hashem commanded the blessing: life forever" (*Tehilim*, 133:3). When he uttered the word *Chayim* / life, he passed away — leaving this world with the word "life" on his lips, joyously passing from one form of life into another.

On Lag b'Omer we don't receive inspiration and revitalization through the medium of a transcendent Yom Tov like Rosh Hashanah or Pesach, rather, we generate it ourselves. This awakening of *Chayim* / life comes from 'below' or within the *natural self*, according to how the 'natural world' functions. We take the initiative with the strength of the *Shor* / bull, the sign of the month, and create our own breakthrough.

This idea of revealing the gift of Hashem in the natural conditions of earthly life is also related to what Rashbi ultimately revealed: the hidden aspects of Torah, also referred to as Kabbalah, or *Sod* / Secret, and later, Chassidus. On Lag b'Omer we thus celebrate the *Matan Penimiyus haTorah* / Giving of the Hidden Aspects of the Torah.

As Lag b'Omer is the beginning of the final third of the Sefirah period, there is already a tangible proximity with Shavuos. Because of this there is a *Reshimu* / imprint, premonition, or reflection of Light from Shavuos, shining backwards in time. The Light of Shavuos is thus reflected within Lag b'Omer. However, this light is not only of the Revealed / Written Torah given on Shavuos; it is also the Light of the Hidden levels of Oral Torah, including especially the Zohar.

The Death of a Tzadik

Normally the time of a person's passing is a time to mourn, to be introspective and serious. In fact, there is an age-old custom to fast on the day of a *Yahrtzeit* / anniversary of passing. The Shulchan Aruch (*Orach Chayim*, 580:1-2) talks about fasting on the seventh of Adar, the day of Moshe's passing, as a sign of mourning. How can we then authentically celebrate on Lag b'Omer, the day of Rashbi's death? There were in fact some sages who were puzzled by the celebration on the day of Rashbi's death (Rabbi Yosef Shaul Nathanson, *Shoel u'Meishiv*. 5, Siman 39). Yes, we know that Rashbi asked that the day he died be a day of celebration, but that may not be enough to actually awaken joy within us. Perhaps it is more natural to be sad on such a day; should we pretend to be happy when we're not? Where does the joy of Lag b'Omer come from?

According to both the Revealed and Hidden levels of Torah, the goal of life in this world is to refine physical matter and reveal the Divine nature of all reality. Life is thus a twofold undertaking: a) refining the world, as well as, b) revealing the Light. The *Nigleh* / revealed aspect of Torah deals more apparently with the refinement of matter, how to operate in this physical world, including the laws of life, ethics, and ritual. The inner aspects of Torah deal more with revealing and channeling Light once our vessel is already refined. Similarly, there are two types of Tzadikim: one who is more involved in the refining of physicality, and the other who is more focused on revealing Light. The "refiner" is more embodied in physical life, and the "revealer" is more at home in the spiritual worlds.

When a "refiner" dies he is still *Mamshich Elokus* / drawing Divinity into the world. However, once he vacates his body, his capacity to interact with and impact the material world greatly decreases. This is because his work and connection in the world was fundamentally focused on refining the realm of physicality. Once he is no longer vested in his body, he is no longer able to be as personally involved with the world. Therefore people mourn his death as he is less present and available than while he was alive.

On the other hand, the life of a "revealer" is primarily a spiritual phenomenon, as he is not deeply attached to his physical needs or desires. This means that there is not a very dramatic decrease in his connection with the world when this Tzadik passes away into the spiritual realms. He was essentially already there. Furthermore, one could even say that not only is there not a significant decrease in a "revealer's" relationship to the world when they die, but their influence can actually grow. While alive, their basic disengagement from physicality resulted in a limitation of their *Hashpa'ah* / influence in the physical world. When the physical body passes away, this limitation is removed and their potential powers of *Hashpa'ah* are greatly increased. Their death can thus awaken great joy and celebration in others, as they will be even more available to students and seekers in far-flung places and future ages.

Rashbi is a Tzadik that is not part of this world (Alter Rebbe, *Siddur Im Dach*, Sha'ar Lag b'Omer. Lubavitcher Rebbe, *Likutei Sichos*, 7 p 335). He is called a *Nuni Yama* / creature of the sea; even while he was in a body he was tucked away in the *Alma d'Iskasiya* / hidden worlds (*Likutei Torah*, Alter Rebbe, Shemini). Ultimately, Rashbi is a Tzadik of the *Penimiyus* / inner dimensions, who did not need to interact directly with people (or even the physical world) in order to accomplish his spiritual mission.

Rashbi's path was to remain completely immersed in Torah contemplation, and not to get involved in any other vocation or work (*Shabbos*, 11a). Many sages tried to live aloof from the world like Rashbi but were unable (*Berachos*, 35b). As he lived wholly in the spiritual realm, he welcomed death — he thus never become attached to this world. His death was therefore more of an anticipated 'release' from the physical realm than a dreaded 'divorce' from it. As he was never really 'in the world' at all, his death was not experienced as a separation, but rather a re-integration.

As the Matan Torah of the hidden levels of Torah, Lag b'Omer is a day of 'revealing Light.' For this reason the day that Rashbi passes is called a *Hilulah* / celebration; as a great Light is revealed.* *Hilulah* also means a wedding celebration. Lag b'Omer is part of the great wedding, or engagement, between us and Hashem.** Shavuos is considered a wedding of sorts. On Lag b'Omer our souls unite spiritually with Hashem, as represented by the Hidden Torah revealed by Rashbi; while on Shavuos our entire being unites with Hashem, as represented by the Revealed Torah of Moshe.

However, this explanation thus far is still framed within a perspective of *duality*; it is not a full expression of the *unity* realized by Rashbi.

---

*Light is associated with joy and celebration: "For the *Yehudim* there was Light and happiness and joy...." Megillas Ester, 8:16. See, *Gittin* 57a.

**This is illustrated by the Halacha that couples may have weddings on Lag b'Omer.

Soon we will delve into a deeper perspective in which death and separation are understood as greater expressions of unity, rather than as forms of disengagement from the world. From this perspective we will be able to understand even more deeply why Rashbi's 'death' is celebrated as a 'wedding' time of unity.

Day of Rashbi

In the writings of the Arizal (*Sha'ar haKavanos*, Pesach, Derush 12. See also *Magen Avraham*, Orach Chayim, 493:3) there is the story of a certain sage who every morning used to recite a prayer for the Temple, lamenting the destruction of Yerushalayim. He did so one day on Lag b'Omer. After he concluded his prayers the Arizal walked over to him and told him that he had seen Rashbi standing near his grave saying, "Why did you say this prayer of mourning on the day of my joy?"

Lag b'Omer is sometimes called *Simchas Rashbi* / the Joy of Rashbi[*]. Rabbi Chayim Yoseph David Azulai (1724 -1806), known as the Chidah (*Avodas HaKodesh*, Morah b'Etzbah, 223), writes that on the day of Lag b'Omer we should increase joy in honor of Rashbi. This is because Lag b'Omer is his *Hilulah* / day of celebration, and it is known that he desired that people should rejoice on this day[**]

---

[*] Another construction of the word *Simchas* is *Samach*, and this is similar to *Shemes*, just with a Ches and not a (similar looking letter) Tav. In many earlier, versions of *Kisvei Arizal*, it says *Samach* or *Simchas*. See, the Chidah, *Maaris HaAyin*, Likutim 7. The Lubavitcher Rebbe, *Igros Kodesh* 3, 485

[**] In the Talmud, *Eiruvin* 54a, *Hilulah* means 'wedding.' In the Zohar, *Hilulah* means the day of a person's passing; *Zohar* 3, 296b. See also *Zohar* 1, 218a.

Let us summarize the reasons that we have already mentioned for celebrating the day of Rashbi's passing, before moving onto any further connections.

The simple reason is that Rashbi asked that this day, his Yartzeit, be celebrated rather than mourned.

Usually, when a Tzadik passes away there is a void left behind, and so the Yahrtzeit has a tone of mourning. However, Rashbi was never attached to this world, so he never really left it. His *Hashpa'ah* / beneficial influence only increased after he was released from the limitations of the body.**

He left behind his son, Rabbi Eliezer, who was equal to him; and in this way lived on (*Sukkah*, 45b. *Shu't Mayim Chayim* of Rabbi Chaim Rappaport, Orach Chayim).

** The Sefirah connected to Lag b'Omer (Hod of Hod) also has the power to defy death and what it represents. Hod is humility (and thanks-giving). Hod of Hod is extreme humility. Experientially, if you feel you are Ayin / no-thing, then there is no-thing that can die. Moshe was on this level of Ayin, as he was "the humblest of all people" [*Bamidbar*, 12:3]. Thus it says that Moshe's body did not decompose (at least not in the manner of other bodies) [*Rashi*, Devarim, 34:7]. The Gemara [*Shabbos*, 152b] tells a story of workers who were digging near the home of Rav Nachman; they found the intact corpse of the Rav Achai bar Yoshiah. Puzzled by the intact, non-decomposed body, Rav Nachman entered into a conversation with the corpse (as the *Maharal* explains, he entered into an internal dialogue with himself and the 'other'). In the course of the conversation, Rav Nachman said to the corpse, "Is it not written, 'And the dust shall return to the earth as it was' (*Koheles*, 12:7)?" The corpse responded, "He who taught you the book of Koheles apparently did not teach you the book of Mishlei, for there (14:30) it states, 'The rotting of bones is [caused by] envy.' This suggests that for one who is envious during life, his bones will rot after his demise, while for one who does not have envy in his heart while alive, his bones will not rot after his demise.

Being humble and grateful, offering thanks for what you have, is a way to integrate the physical body with the eternal soul. On some level, this can allow one to defy the natural dispersion of the elements that comes with the separation of soul and body.

Rashbi was a *Nitzutz* / spark of Adam. The Medrash tells us that the day Adam passed away became a holiday of drinking and joy (*Tana d'Vei Eliyahu*, Chap 16). Therefore, Rashbi's identification with Adam could be why his day of passing is also a celebration.

Rashbi is also considered a *Nitzutz* / spark of Moshe. Yet, the day Moshe passed away did not become a day of celebration, but rather one of mourning. This is for two reasons: a) Moshe is mourned because his life's dream to enter the Land of Israel was not fulfilled; b) when Moshe passed away many laws of the Torah were lost (*Temurah*, 16a). In other words, we mourn when Torah is lost. But when Rashbi passed away more Torah was revealed! The entire *Idra* was revealed on that day (*Sha'ar Yissachar* (Munkach), Chodesh Iyyar. Ma'amar Gal Einai # 23). Additionally, since Rashbi is connected to the *Penimiyus* / inner dimensions and to the *Nistar* / hidden dimensions of the Torah, his 'death' is a celebration, as will be explored.* Whereas Moshe, who openly, brought about the Revelation of the *Nigla* / revealed aspects of Torah (and from a perspective of Nigla we need to mourn on the day of one's passing).

Rashbi was one of the five students of Rabbi Akiva who remained alive after the premature death of the 24,000 students. Unlike the previous students, Rashbi died naturally at a ripe old age and received a proper burial. These are both simple but profound reasons to celebrate.

The day Rashbi died he revealed the Idra, containing many of the great luminous secrets of the Zohar, giving us a reason to celebrate. This is in contrast to Moshe, whose death brought mourning because much Torah was forgotten when he departed (*Temurah*, 16a).

Many people fast on the day of Moshe's death.

It has been suggested that the 33rd day of the Omer is also the day Rashbi and his son left their hideout in the cave (*Aruch haShulchan*, Siman 493:7). This episode is but a piece of the larger narrative of Rashbi's run-in with the Romans, which we will explore in more depth shortly. In short, when Rashbi and his son had been pursued by the Romans they hid in a cave for 12-13 years, and survived under very harsh conditions. However, they used their difficult circumstances as a spiritual retreat, and emerged from the cave in a state of great purity and illumination. Interestingly, the story of Rashbi and his son hiding and then emerging from the cave is recorded on the 33rd page of Gemara Shabbos, subtly linking the story to Lag b'Omer / 33rd day of the Omer. Leaving the cave also represents the end of the horrific aftermath of the Bar Kochva revolt, during which the generation of Rabbi Akiva was persecuted. These too are reasons to celebrate.

It has been intuited that Lag b'Omer is Rashbi's birthday — and thus he died on the same day he was born, just like Moshe (*Bnei Yissaschar*, Iyyar Ma'amor 3. *Pri Tzadik* 3, p. 88).

The 33rd day of the Omer is also the day Rabbi Akiva started teaching Rashbi (Chidah, *Tov Ayin*, 18). Our sages tell us that after the 24,000 students of Rabbi Akiva died, "the world remained desolate until Rabbi Akiva came to our masters in the South and taught the Torah to them." These five students included Rabbi Meir and Rashbi, "...and it was they who revived the [Oral] Torah at that time" (*Yevamos*, 62b). On one level we celebrate the continuation of the Oral Torah, with the successful transmission of the Torah from

Rabbi Akiva to Rashbi and the other four students; but that is only one level. We are also celebrating the increased illumination that Rashbi revealed through the inner dimensions of Torah. From this perspective, not only did the Torah survive, but once Rabbi Akiva passed it on to Rashbi it was in fact revealed on an even deeper level than before.

The 33rd day of the Omer is also the day that Rabbi Akiva gave *Semicha* / Rabbinic ordination to these five new students, including Rashbi of course (*Kaf haChayim,* Orach Chayim, 493:26).

All of these reasons for celebration are intuited as having occurred on the 33rd day of the Omer simply because it is "Rashbi's day." As soon as this day was associated with Rashbi revealing Torah's *Sod* / hidden dimension, any other monumental events in the life of Rashbi would naturally be attributed to *Gal* b'Omer / *Revelation* in the Omer period.

Perseverance and Presence

In addition to celebrating the life, death, and accomplishments of Rashbi, we have also learned a number of reasons why this is likewise a day celebrating the spiritual stamina and rejuvenating *Koach* / power of Rabbi Akiva. Imagine you are one of the greatest teachers of Torah in history, and you have built an army of many thousands of highly talented and righteous students. Then, in your old age, in one very short period, you see all of them die tragic deaths. Realistically, one might think, 'Everything I worked for all these decades is lost; how could I ever even begin to rebuild it at this stage of my life?' Slightly different but similarly, another person might think, 'It is obviously the will of Hashem that I should not transmit my teachings to future generations. Everything the Compassionate One does is for the good; I shall accept this judgment with love.'

Instead, Rabbi Akiva said, 'The world is now *Shameim* / desolate. I will start all over again.' This is why on Lag b'Omer we sing songs about Rabbi Akiva as well as about Rashbi. Lag b'Omer is the 18th, the *Chai* / life of Iyyar because Rabbi Akiva chose life. He did not give up. He was not "idle in the evening" (*Koheles*, 11:6), as Chazal put it; teach students when you are young, and so in the 'evening' when you are older...' *Yevamos*, ibid). After appropriately mourning all of his students, (his entire legacy essentially in ruins) he went right back to work and regenerated the transmission of Torah to his remaining five students. With the strength of a formidable bull, he got up and charged forward.

Additionally, besides both Rabbi Akiva and Rashbi, there is yet another hidden reason why Lag b'Omer is a day of celebration. The Chasam Sofer (*Shu't, Yoreh Deah*, 233) says that it is the day the *Mon* / Manna started falling in the Desert. Other *Mefarshim* / Commentators (*Rashi*, 16:1. *Ba'al Haturim*, Bamidbar, 9:11) write that the Israelites began to receive the Mon on the 15th or 16th of the month, the day their food ran out. Yet, the Chasam Sofer writes, since a person can live three days without food, therefore, the first day the Mon was revealed in the Desert was the 18th of Iyyar. The concept of "living without food" suggests yearning. The Mon as well as the entire time period of Sefirah and Iyyar is focused on yearning and building vessels to receive revelation.

The students of Rashbi once asked him, "Why did the Mon come down every day, and not just once a year?" "I shall give a parable," he replied. "It is like a king of flesh and blood who had an only son, whom he would provide an allowance for food once a year. As a result, the son would visit his father only once a year. Seeing this, the king began to provide his son food every day, so that the son would visit him every day. It is the same with Yisrael. A person who had four or five children would worry, saying: 'Perhaps no Mon will come down tomorrow, and we will all die of hunger.' Consequently, Israel daily turned their attention to their Father in heaven" (*Yuma*, 76a). Thus, the intention of the Mon was that Bnei Yisrael would yearn and constantly turn their attention to receive nourishment from their Divine Provider. This is also the essential dynamic of Iyyar: it is the separation that brings you closer, it is the lack that brings abundance, it is the absence that reveals ultimate presence.

From all the 24,000 students of Rabbi Akiva only five remained to ensure the continual transmission of Torah. Among these five, Rashbi in particular is celebrated as the vehicle for the continuation of the Oral Torah, as well as the revelation of the Hidden Torah. Let us delve more deeply into the context of the story of the 24,000 students, and discover how Rashbi is truly unique.

History of the Rebellion

Let us travel back in history, to the time of Rabbi Akiva. The second *Beis haMikdash* / Holy Temple had been destroyed in 70 CE. Israel lay in ruins. Our People had been ravaged by battle, hunger, persecution, and exceedingly harsh conditions. Hundreds of thousands were exiled and sold into slavery. Titus, the Roman General and son of the newly crowned Emperor, Vespasian, looked upon the land he laid waste and declared that the Kingdom of Judah was no longer. He erected a monument of triumph in Rome known as the Arch of Titus, which still stands today. However, the resilient People of Judea did not give up. Against all logic, they refused to bow to their new state of exile and trauma, and they yearned to return and rebuild Yerushalayim.

Sometime between the years 133 and 135 CE, there appeared a charismatic rebel named Shimon ben Kosiba, known then simply as, "Bar Kosiba." He gathered together a group of Jewish warriors and began to strategize for a war against the Roman occupiers. At first, many of the sages opposed him, but the great Rabbi Akiva was a staunch supporter, seeing him as potentially the Moshiach. One night, Rabbi Akiva had a dream of a rising star, and recognized it as an allusion to the verse, *Darach Kochav m'Ya'akov* / A star shall rise from Ya'akov (*Yerushalmi*, Ta'anis, 4:15). At that point, instead of using his name *Bar Kosiba*, Rabbi Akiva began calling him *Bar Kochva* / Son of the Star.

In the words of the Rambam (*Hilchos Melachim*, 11:3), "…Rabbi Akiva, one of the greatest Sages of the Mishnah, was one of the supporters of King Bar Kosibah and would refer to him as the Messianic King. And not just him but all the sages of his generation considered Bar Kosibah to be the Messianic King until he was killed because of sins. Once he was killed, they realized that he was not the Moshiach." Later, after this failed rebellion, he was called *Bar Kozibah* / Son of deceit.

Rabbi Akiva felt that the exile should not be accepted. He supported the revolt with the hopes that it would usher in the Messianic Era. Clearly, his students would have been instrumental in this revolution, mainly, by transmitting the Torah teachings that would awaken the Jews' capacity for spiritual and physical success. Sensing that Rome might be about to crumble, he felt it was time for the pagan world to adopt the universal principles of the Torah and the Oneness of Hashem. He even envisioned the Jews returning imminently to Israel to build the Third and eternal Temple.

In the beginning, the revolt was somewhat successful. As some sources state, that year, on the 33rd day of the Omer, an amazing event occurred. Bar Kochvah's army — which at its high point has been estimated to be well over a quarter of a million strong — successfully re-conquered Jerusalem. Some suggested that he in fact even began building the Third Temple.

These events, especially as they occurred directly after the destruction of Jerusalem, would have made Rabbi Akiva's belief quite plausible: Bar Kochvah was evidently going to be the Final Redeemer. However, when Bar Kochvah got notice that the Romans had learned of the secret entry way into the fortress at the city of Beitar, he blamed the great sage Rabbi Eliezer for informing them. In a bewildering turn of events, Bar Kochvah had Rabbi Eliezer killed. Rabbi Akivah was utterly stunned, and immediately withdrew his favor and support for Bar Kochvah. This withdrawal of favor was, in a sense, tantamount to a death sentence for Bar Kochvah.[*]

End of the Rebellion

The end of the Bar Kochva revolt was so devastating to Klal Yisrael that it was like the *Churban / destruction of the Temple* all over again. In the words of the Rambam (*Hilchos Ta'anis*, 5:3), speaking about the capture of the city of Betar, the largest city in Israel after the destruction of Jerusalem, "Thousands and myriads of Jews inhabited Beitar. They were ruled by a great king whom the entire Jewish people and the leading Sages considered to be the Messianic King. The city fell to the Romans and they were all slain, *causing a national catastrophe equivalent to that of the Temple's destruction.*"

Hadrian, the Roman Emperor, sent an army made up of six full legions, and elements from up to six additional legions, to crush the revolt. This was much larger than the army that Titus had amassed some 60 years earlier when he destroyed the Beis haMikdash.

After three hard years of battle, with many Roman losses, the Jewish rebellion was brutally crushed in the summer of 135 CE. The Gemara tells us that the most devastating act of Roman vengeance was upon the last Jewish holdout in Beitar. It says the Romans "went on killing until their horses were submerged in blood up to their nostrils" (*Ta'anis*, 4:5), *Rachmana Litzlan /* may the Compassionate One save us.

Looking more deeply at the deaths of the students

---

*See *Sanhedrin*, 93b — 'The Sages killed Bar Kochva.' See also Yerushalmi, *Ta'anis*, 4:5 — 'It was as if the sages killed him, although he physically died from a snake bite.'

In order to more fully understand the spiritual significance of Lag b'Omer, we need to read closer into the manner in which the students died. Chazal tell us 'why they died' (they did not respect each other) as well as how they died of *Askara* / croup,* or something related to choking. But the Sages often speak in metaphors. Was the mention of *Askara* literal, or was it a descriptive metaphor? In the words of Chazal we find both options.

Rav Sharira Gaon (900-1000 CE) of Pumpadissa, Babylon (the father of Rav Hai Gaon) writes in *Igeres Rav Sharira Gaon*, that there was a "religious persecution" during the times of Rabbi Akiva connected with the death of his 24,000 students. This lends weight to the idea that the students died connected or during the Bar Kochva revolt. It also appears from the *Yerushalmi* that they fell in the Bar Kochva revolt, and perhaps died of 'choking.'

Choking could be a metaphor for hunger. Indeed, Bar Kochva himself died when a snake "choked" him (Yerushalmi, *Ta'anis* 4:5).

The Historical Reason for the Period of Mourning: The Shattering of Rabbi Akiva's Dream

Why do we mourn the deaths of the students more than most of the other tragic events in our history — for 32 full days? It is easy to understand why we mourn the destruction of the two Temples and the resulting exiles. Do the deaths of these students really have a greater impact or deserve more attention than the massacres of the Spanish Inquisition, or the Chmielnicki Ukrainian pogroms,

---

* a 'punishment' that is received for Bitul / degrading (the *Kavod*/honor of) Torah, *Shabbos* 33b.

or the Holocaust?

Even more perplexing is the assertion that the students died because they did not have respect for one another. This would seem to suggest that there is less of a reason to mourn them, as they seem unworthy, or maybe even 'deserving' of their death, *Chas veShalom*. Certainly, after 2,000 years why should we mourn them? Wouldn't it be more authentic to turn our attention to more recent and personally felt tragedies?

Torah writings are not meant to be historical only — relating the facts of what happened and when. Torah is primarily a meta-historical teaching that reveals the Divine laws and meanings of life, thereby instructing us how to live in accordance with both creation and Creator. Therefore the Gemara focusses on *why* the students died and what we can learn from their death — for instance, that we must respect each other.

A closer reading unveils a deeper layer. It is not precisely true that the students died because they did not respect each other. No one deserves the 'punishment' of death for lack of respect. Rather, it is like a soldier who takes off his helmet and is struck fatally on his head. He was not 'punished' with the bullet, rather as a consequence of removing his helmet he became vulnerable. With regard to the students, if they would have respected one another, they would have been protected by a 'helmet' of positivity. This lesson may also be received personally, but one can still ask, why do we mourn?

It should be pointed out that despite the horrors of the times, the building of a Third Beis haMikdash was not something beyond the imagining of the Jews. In fact, after the Roman destruction of the Second Beis haMikdash, the Jews had reason to believe that the Romans would allow them to build the Third Temple:

The burning down of the Beis haMikdash by Titus was a "mistake." The Romans did not generally destroy buildings, rather they destroyed peoples. There was no gain for them in burning a useful structure. The Hellenist Jewish historian *Yosifun* / Josephus writes that what happened was a Roman soldier accidentally flung a firebrand into the *Kodesh haK'doshim* / Holy of Holies, and this is what started the unplanned fire. The Maharal counters, "While it may be historically true that it was an accident, from good intentions comes goodness, and from evil intentions comes evil results." The fact that the soldiers of Titus destroyed the Beis haMikdash shows that Titus was a *Rasha* / an evil leader and a 'spiritually blocked' person.

A later Roman Emperor, Julian (362-363 CE), himself actually began constructing a Third Beis haMikdash. Some say that Rav Chilkiyah was against using gentile money to build the Beis haMikdash, and the Jews were anyway ambivalent about the project, but the Emperor nevertheless went ahead with the construction. Apparently it was only due to major earthquakes in Israel that the construction was halted.

On the other hand, what Rabbi Akiva dreamed about was something much more than a mere building. The Final Redemption will not be just another structure, whether physical, social, or even spiritual. It will not merely be a military conquest of territory in the Middle East. When Rabbi Akiva intuited that Bar Kochvah would be the Moshiach, he anticipated a complete paradigm shift from a world of darkness and destruction into a world that would shine like a star of compassion and wisdom. When Bar Kosiba executed Rabbi Eliezer, that dream for the immediate future was shattered. The revolt was crushed, and eventually Rabbi Akiva himself was to be brutally martyred.

This is why we take these tragedies to heart and mourn in this season as a People. We are not just mourning the death of a group of students far back in history, nor for a failed political rebellion. We are mourning the shattering of Rabbi Akiva's dream of redemption. The loss of that dream does indeed affect us personally. All of the difficulties, pogroms, inquisitions, holocausts, anti-semitic attacks, poverty, personal trauma, and illness that we have faced since that time until now would have been prevented by Rabbi Akiva's redemption. Not only that, but all the wars, famines, natural and manmade disasters throughout the world during the last 2,000 years would not have happened, as Creation would have been complete. The failures of the 24,000 students and of Bar Kochva to live according to Rabbi Akiva's principles of mutual respect and honor had cosmic repercussions that all living beings still feel today.

The Historical Reason for Celebrating on the 33rd Day

Rabbi Akiva fought mightily against surrendering to the condition of exile, but it was his student Rashbi who gave us the tools and the understandings of how to live and finally overcome exile. It is Rashbi's teachings that live on after the Bar Kochva failure silenced the teachings of the 24,000 students. Rashbi represents a new start after the shattering of Rabbi Akiva's dream. As we mentioned, the 33rd is the day that Rabbi Akiva started transmitting Torah to his five new students, and it is the day when he finally gave them *Semichah* / ordination to transmit Torah to the next generations.

Rashbi physically survived by taking refuge in a cave. However, his Torah teachings survive and shine upon us because while he was hiding he took the opportunity to turn inward, meditate with uncompromising inner strength, and reveal a hidden light from beyond. Let's look more deeply into this story and its meaning.

Once, as a few of the sages were conversing, Rabbi Yehudah started praising the Roman occupiers for the streets, bathhouses, and bridges that they had skillfully built. Rabbi Yosi remained quiet. Rashbi countered, "All they do they do for themselves alone. They build streets in order to fill them with prostitutes, bathhouses for themselves to bathe, and bridges so they can (get to everyone to) collect taxes. As a result of Rashbi's negative comments about the Roman occupiers, there was, a death warrant put out on his life. At first he hid in the *Beis Midrash* / house of study, but was still worried, so he fled with his son Eliezer and hid in a cave. To avoid the tattering and breakdown of their clothing, they covered their bodies in sand. Miraculously, a spring and a carob tree appeared at the mouth of the cave, providing them with water and food. (Indeed, many have the custom to eat carobs on Lag b'Omer.)

After 12 years of hiding, *Eliyahu* / Elijah the Prophet appeared to Rashbi and told him that the previous Roman emperor was dead. Rashbi stepped out of the cave, and there he saw a person plowing and working the land. Rashbi exclaimed, "Look at these people. They forsake eternity and involve themselves with temporary life!" He was in such a state that whatever he looked at went up in flames. A voice then came from Above saying, "Have you come to destroy My world? Go back into the cave." Rashbi returned and stayed in the cave for another year. Afterward, Rashbi came out of the cave and looked at creation with healing eyes.

At this point in the story we see that: a) Rashbi was a recluse — at least in practice, alone with his son for 13 years with no other contact, and b) he sought "eternal life," the life of the soul. Elsewhere he stated that a person should not work, just have trust in Hashem. He is the paragon of *Toraso Umanuso* / Torah is his only occupation. The Gemara says that many tried to live without a worldly occupation like Rashbi, but were unable to do so (*Berachos*, 35b).

After leaving the cave, Rashbi became a very important teacher and transmitter of the inner teachings of the Torah. At the end of his life, he called together his students and taught them the mysteries of the *Idra*, the deepest parts of the Zohar. On the day he died he asked that his Yartzeit be celebrated.

Rabbi Akiva's paradigm of ultimate redemption perhaps needed to wait a few thousand years, until the coming of Moshiach — when the exile is over — but Rashbi gives us the gift of hope even in exile. Rashbi revealed the light that is present even in darkness. This is the very light which will eventually lead us back to holistic luminosity. As the Zohar states clearly, "With this book (of the Zohar) we will merit to leave exile in mercy" (*Zohar* 3, 124b).

The Zohar — the contemplative, inner teachings of the Torah — is pratically relevant in all ages. In the realm of *Penimiyus* / inner Torah, even when there is no 'external' Beis haMikdash, the internal service is always accessible and effective. If we cannot bring a physical offering to a physical Beis haMikdash, we can bring an internal offering. Therefore the *Penimiyus* allows for the continuation of any and all Mitzvos, even if they are currently not externally applicable or physically feasible.

Similarly, when a person dies physically, it is possible that in a *Penimiyus* way, their life will continue. According to the Zohar, in death a person can be present *Yatir mi'biChayeihu* / even more so than in life. This truth is revealed in the passing of Rashbi. He taught and exemplified the importance of focusing on the *Penimiyus* of life. The day he died is thus a day for celebration of life. As mentioned, this day is called his *Hilulah* / wedding at the same time that it is a day of his *Hillula* / death.

In general, Rashbi is of the opinion that we need to seek out deeper reasons for the Mitzvos. He is *Doresh Ta'amei d'Kra* / he seeks to find the reason for the verse. Finding the deeper significance of Mitzvos is so identified with Rashbi that throughout the Gemara whenever we encounter a passage that looks into the reason for a given Mitzvah, the Gemara immediately identifies it with Rashbi (e.g., *Gittin,* 49b, *Menachos,* 2b, *Sanhedrin,* 16b).

After emerging from 13 years of hiding in the cave, Rashbi met his father-in-law, the saintly Rabbi Pinchas ben Yair.* This is how

---

*The Gemara we are quoting suggests that Rashbi was his son in law, yet, numerous places in the Zohar it is written that Rashbi was his father in law, e.g., *Zohar* 3, 240. Possibly there were two sages with the same name.

the event is described (*Shabbos*, 33b): "Rabbi Pinchas ben Yair heard that his son-in-law had left the cave, and he went out to meet him. He took him into the baths and massaged his flesh. Seeing the cracks in his body, Rabbi Pinchas wept and the tears streamed from his eyes. 'Woe to me that I see you in such a state!' he cried out. 'Happy are you that you see me thus,' Rashbi retorted, 'for if you did not see me in such a state you would not find me thus [learned].'" Rashbi is saying, "Please do not look at the external appearance only; look more deeply. Do not get caught up in superficial perceptions."

The fundamental text of *Sod* / Secret is the Zohar. Just before he passed from this earthly plane Rashbi revealed a body of powerful Torah secrets called the *Idra Zuta* / The Small Threshing Floor — an extremely cryptic section of the Zohar. The revelation of this body of wisdom is but another reason to celebrate this day. The Zohar tells us, "With this book of the Zohar we will merit to leave the exile with mercy."

The teachings of the holy Zohar give us a radiant light that connects our current exile with the coming Redemption. They are a link that connects our present with the deepest present, which is also called the future. They open for us a portal into a time/space/consciousness in which there will be no more mourning, no more harsh Din or concealment, and in which the natural and the supernatural will be unified, all diseases will be eradicated, death will be nullified, and we will celebrate unceasingly.

Deeper reasons why this is a time of Din

Let us go a little deeper. Scanning the sources reveals that Iyyar and the entire Omer period was and is viewed as a time of mourning for numerous reasons, besides the death of the students of Rabbi Akiva.

One of the earliest sources revealing the Din of this period is a teaching in the Mishnah. Rabbi Yochanan ben Nuri says that the sentence of the unrighteous to enter *Gehenom* / purgatory — the transitional 'place' or state of soul cleansing — extends from Pesach to Shavuos (Mishnah, *Ediyos*, 2:10. Although it is important to note that Rabbi Akiva argues with this). This suggests that our mourning is in sympathy for those who have passed from this world and are being cleansed and readied for entry to *Gan Eden* / Paradise (*Shiboley Haleket. Chok Ya'akov*, 439:3). In general this is a time of judgment for souls and because of this we mourn, and as some suggest because of this mourning we do not cut our hair, according to the standard mourning observances (*Imrei Pinchas*, Shabbos U'moadim, 300, 303).

Historically, it appears that the tradition of this time being dedicated to mourning could have originally been a response to blood libels, which often took place around Pesach and thereafter. This also influenced the perception that this is a season of increased *Din* / judgment and harshness for the Jewish people. Victimized communities may have 'mystically/mythically' associated such hardships with the deaths of the students of Rabbi Akiva. In other words, the practices of mourning, such as refraining from getting married, playing music, and cutting hair, may have stemmed from deaths in these later communities. We do know that the early medieval sages associated their own tragedies during this season with the death of the students of Rabbi Akiva (*Otzar Ge'onim* on Yevamos,

62b: *Aruch Hashulchan*, Orach Chayim, 493:1).

The Aruch Hashulchan points out that in medieval times many decrees against the Jewish people were issued during the days between Pesach and Shavuos, such as heavy taxation in France, Germany and so forth (*Orach Chayim* 493:1). Over the centuries, other horrifying persecutions and pillaging also occurred between Pesach and Shavuos.

Among the Ashkenazic communities a strong basis for mourning practices arose with the First Crusade, which began during Sefiras haOmer in 5856 (1096 CE). The Crusades involved groups of non-Jewish religious zealots who set out to conquer Jerusalem and, along the way, killed large numbers of Jews in Ashkenaz. Most of the killing and pillaging happened between Iyyar and the summer. Rabbi Dovid haLevi Segal (c. 1586 - 1667), known as the Taz, wrote that while the (main) custom prohibiting weddings and haircuts until Lag b'Omer commemorates the death of Rabbi Akiva's students, a variant custom of forbidding weddings thereafter until Shavuos laments the tragedy of the Crusades (*Taz*, Orach Chayim, 493:2. See also *Levush*, Orach Chayim, 493:40). For the same reason, according to prevailing Ashkenazic custom, the prayer *Av haRachamim* / Merciful Father, lamenting those killed during the First Crusade, is recited every Shabbos between Pesach and Shavuos, even when that Shabbos also festively blesses the new month (Maharil, *Minhagim*, 21).

The horrific pillaging and murder of Jews, known as the *Gezeiros Tach v'Tat* / Decrees of 1648-49, also known as the Chmielnicki Uprising, took place during this same period. A majority of the uprising took place during the month of April (1648), which in the Hebrew calendar is around Iyyar.

Essentially, the Chmielnicki Uprising was a Cossack rebellion in the Ukraine, aspiring to liberate Ukraine from Poland. It was headed by a Cossack named Hetman Chmielnicki (pronounced *Khmelnitsky*), who together with the Crimean Tatars and local peasants, battled the forces of the Polish (Lithuanian) commonwealth, with the ultimate aim of creating an autonomous Ukrainian state.

Whether it was to arouse the peasantry to battle the Poles, or just out of pure anti-Semitic hatred, Chmielnicki rallied the peasants with an anti-Semitic battle cry. Most Polish magnates lived in Poland proper, and sold or leased certain privileges to their arendators (lease holders or property managers), many of whom were Jews. As the Polish magnates themselves did not supervise their estates, the task of collecting rental and tax payments fell upon the arendators, and this made the Jewish arendators an easy target of hatred and subterfuge. Chmielnicki inflamed the peasant hatred by publicizing a lie that the Poles had sold the estates to the Jews. The Cossacks and peasants then joined forces to massacre tens of thousands of Jews and destroy and pillage hundreds of Jewish communities.

Tens of thousands of Jews were massacred, and literally hundreds of communities were destroyed and pillaged during this dreadful period. The losses inflicted on the Jews of Poland during this period were appalling and colossal. Rabbi Ya'akov Emden notes these devastating losses in his Siddur (*Beis Ya'akov*), "During the Sefirah period Rabbi Akiva's students died, and a number of communities were also destroyed at the same time of year during the Crusade in Ashkenaz and in 1648 (or '49) in Poland."

Due to these extraordinary events throughout history, many understood that the Sefirah period is a time of harsh judgment in general. Although these events seem to hint at something deeper — a mysterious, almost sinister, seasonal energy playing out throughout history.

Chazal tell us that the period from Pesach to Shavuos is a time of judgment with regard to vegetation; indeed there is actually a *Din* / judgment on the *Tevuah* / wheat or grain harvest on Pesach (*Mishnah*, Rosh Hashanah 1:1. See also *Chok Ya'akov*, Orach Chayim 439:3). In other words, on Pesach there is a Divine judgment on how plentiful the produce of the coming year will be, and on Shavuos there is a similar judgment on the fruits of the trees (*Rosh Hashanah*, 16a). This is the reason why the Omer offering was brought to the Beis haMikdash on Pesach: to create, on its day of judgment, a positive influence upon the abundance of the produce of the year. Similarly, we bring a New Meal offering and new fruits on Shavuos because it is a day of Judgment for the fruits of the tree.

As mentioned, a judgment of the unrighteous in Gehenom is also said to occur during this period. This idea can possibly be linked with the notion of the judgment of vegetation. The Arizal (*Sha'ar haGilgulim*, Hakdamah, 22) teaches that a human soul that needs to reach its *Tikkun* / soul elevation by coming back to the world, may sometimes transmigrate into a plant, tree, or fruit. Then, their elevation back into human reality can be accomplished during the first few months of spring. To explain, for some souls, in order to re-attain their perfected state and enter Gan Eden they need to return to the world for a period of time in a different life form.

In the natural world, as opposed to in human life, there is no conflict between the desires of the body and the soul. For example, the instincts of plants are reactive, unmediated by will or choice. The reason for this is that the Creator has already chosen everything for them. A human soul, by residing temporarily within a plant, achieves its Tikkun by submissively manifesting the will of the Creator and getting in touch with its own true nature. The elevation of human souls residing within vegetation occurs during the first months of the spring. Based on this, it could be suggested that the judgment on wheat is connected to the souls who are in a *Gilgul* / reincarnation or transmigration in stalks of wheat.

"On Shavuos there is a judgment on the fruit of the tree" (*Rosh Hashanah*, 16a). According to the *Mekubalim* / Kabbalists (*Tola'as Ya'akov*. See also *Shaloh, Meseches Shavuos*, Ner Mitzvah), the word 'tree' is a conceptual reference to the Creator, and 'fruit' refers to souls. Thus on these days there is a judgment on human souls, which are but fruits connected to the cosmic Tree of Life. This connects again to the judgment of souls during this season in general, and perhaps specifically to the souls that are reincarnated into fruit.

One of the early *Rishonim* / Early Commentators, Rabbeinu Yerucham (1290-1350), states simply that the period between Pesach and Shavuos is one of Din (see; *Toldas Adam*, Nesiv 5:4). This is perhaps connected with the teachings of our Sages, that between Pesach and Shavuos we need to protect ourselves from negative 'winds' and influences. According to this perspective, the reason we would wave the Omer offering in all directions, is that this motion created a protective space around us unaffected by the negative winds present during this particular time (*Menachos*, 62a. *Medrash Rabbah*, Vayikra, 28:3).

All of the above examples of judgment and harsh decree become manifest outwardly because inwardly this is a time of judgment. However, we still need to ask why; what is the meta-story that gives rise to the death of the students of Rabbi Akiva, to the Crusades and other massacres, and to the judgment of souls?

The Meta-Reason

From a perspective of *Pirud* / separation, every given reason seems to be distinct, or even in competition with the others. For instance, one reason behind the Din of this time is the death of the students of Rabbi Akiva. A different reason is because of medieval anti-Semitic persecutions. A competing reason it that it is a time of judgment in Gehenom and so forth. From a perspective of *Yichud* / unity, all valid reasons express a singular intent, and each different reason is only reflecting a different vantage point on the singular truth.

The Omer is a Time of **Katnus / Constriction**

In the 16th century the Arizal revealed even deeper levels of insight into this period of Din and *Katnus* / smallness or constriction (*Sha'ar haKavanos*, Derush 12, Sefiras haOmer. *Maamorei Admur HaZaken*, Parshios, 2, p. 593). For example, the custom of not cutting hair is connected not only with 'mourning' the deaths of the students of Rabbi Akiva (The Chidah, *Avodas HaKodesh*, Morah b'Etzbah, 221), but with the spiritual quality of *Katnus* itself. In fact, the reason the students of Rabbi Akiva, whose souls were rooted in *Gevurah shebeKatanus* / severity of constriction (and the number 24 is also connected to Din, *Torahs Levi Yitzchak* [by the father of the Lubavitcher Rebbe] p. 17), and who acted towards each other in Katnus (smallness/pettiness, with no respect), died during this time period is because it is a time of intense *Katnus*. Even in the material world, (*Imrei Pinchas*, Shabbos uMoadim, 301-302), there is a Katnus of financial difficulty during this time period.

From this perspective, the Omer is not a time of mourning per se, but rather a time of constricted consciousness. Following the initial *Gadlus* / expansiveness and freedom given to us on the night of Pesach, *Gadlus* is removed and we necessarily descend into a relatively constricted, confused state. What goes up must come down, and on Pesach we were elevated to the highest heights. Hence, it is only natural that we experience a 'come-down' following such an uplift. The goal of Sefiras haOmer is thus to gradually make our way back up that mountain, so to speak, step by psycho-spiritual step.

Following Pesach we therefore reside in and move through various degrees of Katnus until Shavuos, when we receive an influx of Gadlus again, but this time in a much deeper and higher, transformative, integrated and compassionate way. The Arizal calls this *Gadlus Shelishi* / third-level expansiveness, where Tiferes is unified with and transmitting light from Keser. Throughout the Omer period we are refining and building our 'vessels' made of the desire to receive this Gadlus, so that when it finally descends it is truly appreciated and assimilated, and not merely taken for granted as just another 'gift' from Above.

From Katnus to Gadlus

The *Katnus*-then-*Gadlus* process is replicated throughout all of creation. The process of creation itself occurs via a *Katnus* / constriction, which is also termed *Tzimtzum* / withdrawal of the Infinite Light of the Creator, followed by a movement of *Gadlus*, an expansion of light and creativity. Ever since that original process of creation, the sequence and rhythm of *Katnus* / smallness to *Gadlus* / expansiveness is present within everything and every process. Similarly, before every birth, there must be a contraction. Before a state of maturity, there needs to be a stage of immaturity, before illumination, there must be darkness, before release, tension. We also see this dynamic at play in terms of the holidays; before the festive day of Purim there is a fast day, *Ta'anis Ester*. Before the celebration of Pesach there is a fast of the first born. Fasting is *Katnus*, and feasting is *Gadlus*.

Commensurate with the degree of *Katnus* is the degree of *Gadlus* that follows. For example, the development of an animal is very different than the development of a human being. Within an hour after birth, many animals are fully developed; "A day old ox is called an *ox*" (*Baba Kama*, 65b). There is a small difference between a baby elephant and an adult elephant, besides their size. A small elephant is a complete elephant, just in miniature and with less physical strength. A lizard is already independent when it hatches and ready to seek its prey, without any need for parental nurturance.

A human being, by contrast, is the slowest developing 'animal.' It takes years before a child learns to walk and talk, let alone fend for itself. The *Katnus* of a human being is much lower than other life forms, but the *Gadlus* of the human being is correspondingly higher. After much development, a human being can choose to perform intellectually complex tasks beyond or even against his instinctual patterning.

The same is true in reverse; the higher the Gadlus, the lower the subsequent stage of Katnus. When the Gadlus, the life-force, of a fruit leaves the fruit, it slowly rots and enters a state of Katnus. The smell of rotting fruit is much less intense than the smell of a rotting animal carcass — the Katnus of an animal is thus lower than the fruit. The odor of a rotting dead animal is arguably less foul than that of a rotting human corpse, as a human has an even lower Katnus. Similarly and perhaps most tellingly, the laws of *Tumah* / impurity, another form of Katnus, are much more stringent in relation to a human body than to an animal. When higher Gadlus is removed, the resulting Katnus is much lower.

On the night of the Pesach Seder in the month of Nisan we receive a powerful revelation of *Gadlus Rishon* / first level expansiveness, but, because it comes to us as a miraculous gift from Above, with very little effort on our part, we cannot fully integrate it. Pesach represents a quantum leap in spiritual stature, we are Divinely catapulted from the 49th level of impurity to a high level of purity. We simply do not have the vessels at this point to integrate and assimilate so much light in a sustainable way. As a consequence, we soon descend into a deep level of Katnus, as the light returns, leaving us liberated but lost and confused. During Iyyar we are therefore in a state of Katnus and are working to raise ourselves up to a higher stage of Gadlus. In the subsequent month of Sivan we receive the Torah, which is Gadlus from the level of Keser, in a way that we can actually integrate. As such, prior to the Gadlus of *Matan Torah* / the Giving of the Torah we have to build vessels to receive and integrate it. We do this through the constrictive effect of judgment, yearning, and courageous inner work.

The word *Katan* / small comes from the two letter root word *Kat* / broken or cut, as in *Katua*. The word *Gadol* comes from the two-letter root word *Gad* (Gimel-Dalet), which means continuation or extension, as in the extension of the hand of a *Gomel* / giver, as he is giving to the *Dal* / poor person, the receiver (*Shabbos*, 104a). This suggests unifying or grouping, especially when this root appears in the word such as *Aguda*; as in *Aguda Achas* / one (unified) congregation, and in *Lo Tisgodedu* / the prohibition not to make separate groupings. In the language of Chazal as well, *Gad* means connecting or continuing, as in the phrases *Gud Asik* and *Gud Achis* / the wall extends upwards or extends downwards.

This is the basic difference between a *Katan* and a *Gadol*, an immature and a mature person. An immature person is disjointed, scattered, and splintered. A mature person is 'continuous' or whole, aligned and inwardly unified with his deepest self. Part of our *Avodah* / inner work during the month of Iyyar is to connect and unify the days as we are counting them. Counting involves gathering details and singular, separate entities (one, two, three), and unifying them into a greater collective, the sum total. Counting the days of the Omer helps us gradually move out of Katnus — a constricted, disjointed state — into the Gadlus of Shavuos.

Our sages tell us (*Megilah*, 31b), "Ezra (the Scribe) instituted that we read from the Torah the curses in Vayikra before Shavuos, and the curses in Devarim before Rosh haShanah. What is the reason? So that *the year may end along with its curses.*" In other words, we read the 'curses' at the end of the year, in order that any curses or unresolved issues should be resolved so that we may start anew. Our sages continue, "Granted, with regard to the curses in Devarim it is so you can say, 'so that the year should end along with its curses.' But as regards those in Vayikra — is Shavuos a New Year? Yes! Shavuos is also a New Year, as we have learnt, 'Shavuos is the new year for (the fruit of) the tree.'"

There are 49 curses in the Book of Vayikra. Parenthetically, in the Book of Devarim there are double that number, 98, which is fitting as Devarim is the 'repetition of the Torah' (see *Tosefos*, Gittin, 2a). The 49 days of the Omer are the cleansing for the 49 curses, which come as a result of sin, and general Katnus. Then comes the 50th day, the Gadlus and the Giving of the Torah, where we are beyond all sin and smallness. When the Gadlus of Shavuos comes there is a ceasing of all 'curses' and a completely new beginning.

It is not only a new year for (the fruit of) the tree, but also for a new you. We ourselves are reborn in the Gadlus of Shavuos. In the words of our sages (Yerushalmi, *Rosh Hashanah*, 4:8), "With regards to all the offerings (in the Temple) the Torah uses the word *Chet* / sin offering, but this is not so with the offering on Shavuos." Here, the Torah refers to the offering as *Se'ir Izim* / goats. Why? Hashem says to Klal Yisrael, 'Since you accepted the yoke of Torah, I will consider it as if you have never sinned.' Shavuos is like a new year for us because we, the fruit of the tree, begin again. We no longer have any record of past negativity or smallness. We are allowed to enter into our own maturity, aligned and unified with our own *Gadlus* / limitless potential.

Embracing Katnus

Insofar as the Omer period gives us an experience of the Katnus prior to a new level of Gadlus, and the 'curses' preceding greater blessings, we can understand that it is extremely important to accept and honor the Katnus. We cannot bypass the process or try to push aside Katnus to jump to Gadlus. For example, when a person experiences the death of a loved one and the extreme Katnus that comes with such a devastating event, this person needs to stop and be *Dom* / silent. Only after a mourner has the chance to be present in their silence and aloneness for a few days can healing begin. Gradually the mourner shifts back into conversation, regular activities and a state of relative expansiveness begins to return. If we do not take our time to sit in our Katnus and mourn properly, real healing may be blocked and an inner wound may fester and cause even more harm later on.

Similarly, we need to support others as they go through their own process of contraction and then gradual expansion. This is why, for example, we have a custom of refraining from initiating conversations with someone who is in the first stages of mourning. This is a gesture of respecting their totally natural experience of Katnus. By not forcing them to expand beyond where they are comfortable or pulling them out of their own internal process, we help hold the space within which a mourner can feel safe to be 'small' or contracted into themselves.

In order to support the vital experience of Katnus during the Omer period, we refrain from getting married, utilizing festive music as a means of expansion, or stimulating a sense of inner refreshment by cutting our hair. Essentially, we act like mourners and focus inward before coming back out to reconnect to the world. If we do not embrace Katnus when it naturally presents itself, it may reappear later in distorted or unexpected ways (although see Rabbi Meir of Apta, *Ohr laShamayim,* Parshas Emor). The energy of Katnus within the body and consciousness needs to be released in the right way with intentionality and purpose, or it can leak out in the form of physical, emotional, mental, or spiritual malaise — even possibly in disease. Rebbe Pinchas of Koritz (*Imrei Pinchas,* Sha'ar 3, 161-162), once had a student who complained that he was suffering from constipation, a form of Katnus and restriction on a physical level. The Rebbe told him that this symptom came about because instead of embracing Katnus when it arose, he pushed it away, ignored it, resisted it, and tried to sweep it under the rug. His suggestion to the student was to fast and to embrace the experience of Katnus. This, he said, would bring him to a proper and healthy state of expansion.

We can now understand that the period between Pesach and Shavuos is characterized by a Din that is not limited to any one of the previous reasons given, such as the death of the students of Rabbi Akiva, the various persecutions and massacres at this time, nor even the seasonal judgment in Gehenom. The underlying meta-reason for all these forms of Din is primarily because this time period is characterized by the quality of Katnus.

Let's now explore more deeply what it is that gives rise to cosmic Katnus in the first place. This will help us understand the Divine purpose of Katnus in our lives, which will then allow us to embrace and engage Katnus, when appropriate or necessary in the context of our souls' development.

The Dynamic Structure of the Spring Months

To begin, we need to review the basic structure of the first three months of the year. The first month is Nisan, the month of redemption, freedom from exile. The third month of the year is Sivan, in which we receive the Torah at Mount Sinai. In Nisan we move out and away from *Mitzrayim* / Egypt and its *Meitzarim* / the narrow constraints of exile that immobilize us physically, mentally, and spiritually; this is 'freedom from…' In Sivan, as we will shortly explore, we receive the 'freedom *to*…'— this is the freedom to choose a new reality. We receive the revelation of a structured wisdom / teaching that allows us to continuously choose freedom, and to integrate it and act on it. It is not enough to let go of the old or break out of what feels like constraint. Nor is it sufficient to be free *from*; to get out of jail, to be redeemed from negativity, or to leave behind a harmful relationship or job. To be authentically free, we must also choose a new positive reality and engage with a path that supports us in living with this new reality.

Iyyar is the bridge between Nisan and Sivan, between 'freedom from' and 'freedom to.' In Iyyar we have already been freed from our old, narrow world of alienation and exile, but we have not yet received the Torah, our new reality and path. Thus we yearn and count the days until we receive it. The longing and counting creates *Kelim* / vessels so that the Torah we receive in Sivan will be properly absorbed and integrated.

This waiting period is full of yearning and anticipation, but at the same time, patience. In the Zohar, the term for this is *Katir* / waiting, as in *Katir Li Za'ir* / wait for me a moment. *Katir* (the Hebrew root word would be Kat, as in Katnus) has the same letters as *Keser* / crown, the highest of the *Sefiros*. If we wait patiently and work productively within the Katnus of our spiritual needing and yearning, we will eventually receive the 'crown' of Gadlus that we need in order to grow and become who we are meant to be. As our yearning has created proper vessels, we will be able to assimilate this revelatory gift from Above.

On the very first day of Sivan we arrived at Mount Sinai and were unified in community "like one person with one heart" (*Shemos* 19:1-2, *Rashi*). This *Gadlus* made us ready to receive the one Torah of *Hashem Echad* / the One G-d. At that moment we no longer were limited to 'freedom *from*'; we were given the 'freedom *to*' choose a higher way of being and living.

Imagine a person is in an abusive relationship, or a teenager is stuck with bad friends. Imagine you have the power to pull them out of their situation and force them from their personal Egypt — for example to take the teenager out of the school or the harmful situation. In many instances this is a necessary first step. However, another step is essential: to integrate them into a new healthy place and structure. If they merely have 'freedom *from*' the harmful situation, without 'freedom *to*' grow within positive surroundings, in time they will revert back to their old patterns and relationships, because those constitute the only framework they know.

Even if you were to tell the teenager, "This group of friends is not good for you. Here, hang out with these other people instead;" and the teenager accepted your reasoning and tried to comply, it still might not be successful. If the teenager does not independently desire to become part of the new group of friends, or have the drive to forge new relationships, he or she may revert back to the old group. To successfully move from one condition to the other, the teenager needs an intermediary stage, in which they build their 'vessels' by 1) embracing the discomfort of change, and 2) realizing their own inner desire for the new reality.

Without such an intermediary stage, the *Gadlus*, clarity, and openness that we receive by 'leaving constraints' and letting go, is usually transient and fleeting. This is why, following the brilliant Gadlus of Seder Night, "the night that shines brighter than day," we immediately plummet into Katnus, and begin the counting of the Omer the very next night.* So many people feel some type of high on the Seder night, only to wake up the next morning feeling low again, and maybe even lower than before. In stark juxtaposition to the Gadlus of the night before, is the acute sense of Katnus the following day. And as we enter the stage of semi-mourning or introspection that characterizes the Sefirah period, we begin to yearn for our vessels to receive Gadlus on a level that is even deeper than the night of Pesach. We thus prepare for the the night of Shavuos.

---

* Outside of Israel, where a Seder is celebrated on the second night, we nonetheless count the Sefirah. Some count even before the Seder in accordance with the custom of the Ra-

Accordingly, the more we yearn to receive the revelation of Torah and desire to follow its paths, the more it will be absorbed and assimilated into our consciousness when we finally receive it.

To summarize, there are three stages in integrating freedom: a) 'freedom *from*' or eliminating the old negative path, b) 'building vessels' by embracing Katnus and creating a desire for the new positive path, c) 'freedom *to*' or choosing to live committedly within the new positive paradigm.

Theoretically, Shavuos should have occurred right after Pesach; the eighth day of Pesach should have been the *Atzeres* / the completion of this process of illumination, just like the *Atzeres* of Sukkos comes seven days after Sukkos. The Torah would then have been given on the eighth day after the People left Egypt, the day after the Splitting of the Sea. This did not happen. Due to the circumstances, the Torah had to be given after seven full weeks (not just seven days) had passed. If the People would have received it after only seven days, they would not have been ready. Their vessels, which are rooted within their desire to receive, would not have been strong enough. It would have been an unsuccessful attempt to leap from stage 'a' to stage 'c.' They would thus not have successfully entered the stage of 'freedom *to*,' represented by the acceptance of the Torah.

---

shash (*Nahar Shalom*, 32b) and the Alter Rebbe. Other Mekubalim such as the Chidah and the Mahara m'Panu suggest that we can only enter Katnus and count the Sefirah, after the Gadlus of the second Seder. In any case, the second Seder is an enactment of Chazal. Therefore, the Gadlus of the second Seder is a Gadlus from Chazal.

The Katnus of Spiritual 'Niddah'

In order to dig deeper into these psycho-seasonal dynamics we will now introduce a new lens through which we can observe and interpret the significance of this unique time period. Previously, we viewed the month of Iyyar through the metaphor of a developing child, as well as in the context of mourning. Now we will construct an entirely different frame through which to understand these elemental energies — that of the lover and spouse.

It is important to note that these different metaphors, that of the child or of the spouse, are not mutually exclusive. Our relationship with Hashem is multi-dimensional and constantly changing. Sometimes we relate to Hashem as our Divine Parent, while other times we relate to Hashem as our passionate Lover or committed Spouse. Both of these paradigms can be found throughout Torah and Rabbinic literature. Iyyar just so happens to be a time period that draws upon both of these relational dynamics in different ways. We will therefore take time to develop them both in this text.

The rhythms of marital life are primarily based on alternating periods of distance and desire, as well as closeness and connection. Therefore, another way of looking at Iyyar, the intermediate stage of embracing Katnus in between the *Gadlus* and *Yichud* of Pesach and Shavuos, is to compare it to the time when a wife is in *Niddah* / temporarily separate from her husband during her menses. From this perspective, both Iyyar and the Omer Period in general can be understood as a time of self-reflective separation in the context of a loving relationship; a kind of 'taking some alone time' in preparation for a deeper and higher unification.

After leaving Egypt, the Israelites experienced *Tumah* / an inner blockage or closure, for reasons which we will explore shortly. As a result, seven weeks were required to gradually reopen their vessels in order to productively receive. During the Omer period we too are, so to speak, temporarily distanced and blocked from being illuminated or 'impregnated' by Hashem. We need an extended time to be separate, to turn inward, cleanse ourselves of any blockages, and finally to open our hearts and minds to again be intimate with our Divine Spouse, this time at Mount Sinai.

Some sages refer to these seven weeks between Pesach and Shavuos as *Chol haMoed* / intermediate festival days (*Ramban* and *Rabbeinu Bachya* on Vayikra 23:36, regarding the era of the Beis haMikdash). Normally, the festive atmosphere of Chol haMoed cancels the mourning practices of someone who has lost a relative. We see from this that the Omer period is not exactly a time of mourning. It is for sure an introspective period, a time of seriousness and Teshuvah. However, instead of seeing ourselves as a mourner during this time, lamenting the many losses of Jewish history, we can visualize ourselves as a Wife who is preparing to return to her Husband.

Yearning, longing, and desiring are terms that suggest separation. Meaning, one has not yet arrived, or is in some sense separate from where they want to be or who they want to be with. One of the inner reasons for the Torah's laws of Niddah, says Rashbi himself, is to create a stronger desire between spouses (*Niddah*, 31b). Something that is always available becomes stale, routine, and taken for granted. Indeed, the practice of temporary separation is to help make room for a greater longing and thus more passionate unity. This "separation that brings you closer" is one of the primary dynamics present within the Omer period and the month of Iyyar, as we journey from one closeness (Pesach) to an even higher intimacy (Shavuos).

Tumah, often translated as 'impurity,' is not really a hygienic issue, and it is certainly not a judgmental term. The word comes from a root meaning 'closed off' (*Yuma*, 39a), blocked, or separated. It is always a condition connected to some form of death, separation, or stagnation of energy. In terms of menstrual Niddah, the Tumah results from a missed opportunity to become pregnant; insofar as the previous intimacy did not produce a new life, it is as if there was a small experience of 'death.' Some time is required to recover from this loss and to regenerate the openness for a new opportunity. Thus, a woman who has menstruated 'counts seven clean days' between the end of menstruation and the time she can again become 'ritually pure' or open to giving life.

Seen from this perspective, we can understand how Iyyar is thus associated with Niddah, a state of separation from Divine intimacy (*Zohar* 3, 97a-b. *Ohr HaChayim*, Vayikra, 23:15). Just as a wife counts seven days, we count seven weeks between our leaving the impurity and blockage of Egypt and the giving of the Torah of life.* The Din of Iyyar is therefore feeling the separation, Katnus, and yearning of a Niddah. We feel that we have not yet arrived at the goal that

---

*Regarding the similarity of the days of the Omer and the seven days of a couple's separation, the Radziner writes that in Parshas Tazria-Metzora, where the laws of Niddah are delineated in Chapter 15:13-15, there are 49 words and the 33rd word is *Moed*, which is also translated as 'holiday,' alluding to the 33rd day of the Omer, the holiday of Lag b'Omer.

Pesach had presented. We burn with an intense longing to cleanse ourselves, to clear ourselves of blockages, and to reach Sinai, where we will be in a state of higher unity with Hashem.*

Pre-Birth Niddah vs. Post-Birth Niddah

Generally speaking, there is a monthly rhythm of Niddah, defined by when a woman menstruates. We can call this 'pre-birth' Niddah. However, there is also a state of Niddah which comes after a birth. The month of Iyyar is more similar to the post-birth Niddah.

As we have explored, the birth of Klal Yisrael occurs with the Exodus in Nisan.** First there are plagues — the birth pangs or contractions which help push us out of the confining 'womb' of Egypt.

---

* This is the inner reason why we do not recite the *Shehechiyanu* blessing on the Mitzvah of counting the Omer. *Shehechiyanu* is recited to celebrate and give thanks for special occasions and new and unusual experiences, such as a Mitzvah that is performed only once year. There are various reasons offered in the Rishonim for why we do not recite this blessing on each night of the Omer (see, *Ba'al Ha'Maor*, Pesachim, 28a). The Kedushas Levi writes that the Omer is a 'countdown,' much like a woman's counting of seven days. The joy is only on Shavuos, the time of *Yichud* / unity (*Bnei Yissaschar*, Nisan, 12:11. *Imrei Pinchas*, Shabbos u'Moadim, 308).

** Going out of Egypt is the process of childbirth, thus post –birth status. In Torah law, there is a period of 33 days following the birth of a male and 66 days following the birth of a female, in which the mother has a unique status (*Vayikra*, 12; 3- 5). The number mid-way between 33 and 66 is 49, perhaps, another reason for the 49 days of Sefirah.

Then we exit the womb on Pesach Night. Finally, with the parting of the waters on the Seventh Day of Pesach, we pass through the 'birth-canal' of the sea, until we finally emerge and are born as a nation.*

As you may have noticed, in this narrative, we play more than one role. On the one hand, as we spoke about in previous chapters, we are identified with the child being born in Nisan, and we are dutifully working our way towards maturity and acceptance of the Torah at Sinai. On the other hand, we are the pregnant and laboring mother giving birth with Hashem, as it were, our highest collective potential. From this vantage point, during the seven weeks that follow the birth of Klal Yisrael on Pesach, we are like the mother of the child, experiencing 'seven days' of post-birth Niddah.

From this perspective, the entire process of leaving Egypt, receiving the Torah, and entering the land of Israel begins with a state of 'Pre-birth Niddah.' This is the Egyptian Exile, in which we are experientially separated from our deeper selves, from our Land, and from our Beloved Hashem. This separation is a form of *Tumah*

---

* On Pesach night there is such a great revelation of unity; why after Pesach do we need to count seven weeks and then purify ourselves so that there can be unity again on Shavuos? This is essentially the question that the holy Arizal asks (*Pri Eitz Chayim*, Sha'ar Chag haMatzos, 1). It is brought down in the Poskim (*Birkei Yoseph*, Orach Chayim, Siman 240:13) that according to Sod, the night of *Shevi'i Shel Pesach* / the Seventh of Pesach is an appropriate time for Yichud or *Zivug* / coupling, uniting. This means that on Pesach Night there is Gadlus, unity, and an absence of Tumah. The next night, however, the Tumah returns. Pesach is the 'birth' of Klal Yisrael, and thus there is an after-effect of Tumah for seven days — the seven days of Pesach and the *Shivah Neki'im* / the seven days of cleansing and preparation for reunion. On *Shevi'i shel Pesach*, as we cross through the Yam Suf it is as though we immerse in a Mikveh, and return to Taharah again. In practice, however, we need seven weeks, not days, to purify ourselves for the higher Yichud. Thus, the element of Mikveh is attained on Shavuos Night as well. Indeed, there is a Minhag [from the Zohar] to 'adorn the Bride' through Torah study on Shavuos Night, and to immerse ourselves in a Mikveh just before dawn.

/ impurity, blockage, stagnation. Indeed, as mentioned earlier, the Sages teach that we had sunk to the 49th level of Tumah in Egypt. Then, miraculously, there is a remembering of who we really are, and a crying out to Hashem from the pain of our slavery. In response to our cries, Hashem 'remembers' us as well. This is the seed of redemption, followed by a process of gestation, birth, separation, purification, and reunification on a higher level than before.

In this way, we are first the estranged lover in Egypt, then the 'remembered' wife, the pregnant and laboring mother, the solitary and self-reflective Niddah, and finally the prepared and purified bride at Sinai. Each of these relationship paradigms serve a purpose in our narrative of redemption and illumination. At first we are the estranged lover, exiled in the Tumah of Egypt. We are then remembered by Hashem, His love for us is rekindled, and He takes us out of our external and internal slavery. In the process, we become pregnant with the potential to receive and reveal more light than we ever thought possible. This gestational phase climaxes in the dramatic birth of Klal Yisrael, our highest collective purpose, and is then followed by a period of isolation and inner work. Finally we arrive at the foot of the mountain ready to receive the Infinite Light of our Beloved Hashem.

We will now explore this process in more depth.

Intimate Reunion

The onset of the exile in Egypt begins with the death of Yoseph. As the Torah tells us, "Now, Yoseph died…. And a new king arose over Egypt, who did not know Yoseph." In the very next verse it says, "He said to his people, 'Behold, the people of the Children of Israel are more numerous and stronger than we....' So the Egyptians enslaved the children of Israel with back-breaking labor" (*Shemos*, 1:6-13). When Yoseph is about to die he calls over his brothers and tells them, "I am going to die. Hashem will surely remember you and take you up out of this land…" (*Bereishis*, 50:24). The phrase Yoseph uses, "will surely remember you" is *Pakod Yifkod* פקד יפקד. This type of remembrance suggests knowledge in the sense of intimacy. When our sages advise a husband to be physically intimate with his wife before he goes on a trip, they say *Lifkod es Ishto* / to be intimate with his wife (*Yevamos*, 62b, *Rashi*. For a different perspective, see *Tosefos*, ad loc. Rashba, *Toras haBayis*, 7:2).

As such, the act of Hashem 'remembering' us in Egypt, the beginning of our redemption, is similar to a husband 'remembering' his wife and being intimate with her. Our sages tell us that there was a secret signal transmitted to the Jewish people to discern if their time of redemption was near. When a leader arose claiming to be the redeemer, if he would proclaim the words *Pakod Yifkod*, this would be a sign that he was the true redeemer of Klal Yisrael, and that their redemption was immanent.*

We therefore see that the key word signaling the beginning of redemption is a word that represents deep intimacy, connection, and reunion. Exile is alienation, separation, a time of Niddah, being cut off from oneself, from other loved ones, and from the Source

---

* *Medrash Rabbah*, Shemos, 3:8. *Targum Yonasan*, Bereishis 50:24. *Rashi*, Shemos 3:18. Moshe had a speech impediment, specifically he says that he has *Aral Sefasayim* / 'closed

of Life. Redemption is a reunion, a *Pakod* / remembrance, and an intimate embrace.

Conception and Pregnancy

The moment Hashem 'remembers' us in Egypt is the moment of unity. This unity leads to conception. We are thus simultaneously conceived as a people, as well as impregnated with the Divine calling of birthing our highest self in sacred community.

In Egypt we were like a fetus in a mother's womb, says the Medrash (*Mechilta*, Beshalach 6); while the Arizal says that in Egypt we were in a condition of *Ibbur* / pregnancy (Shaar *haKavano*s, Derushei Pesach, 1). We can see from these two sources that we are both in utero and 'with child.' In the womb, first we grow into an embryo. At this stage, our life as a people is only potentially viable. When Moshe, who refers to himself as the midwife of Klal Yisrael, appears on the scene we become a viable fetus and a more confident and hopeful mother-to-be. Thus from his appearance until the actual Exodus from Egypt is the *Ibbur* / pregnancy proper. While at this point we may have a more viable existence, we are still in a hidden form, growing gradually within our deepest selves.

In our last moments in Egypt we were asked to offer a *Korban Pesac*h / Paschal Lamb to mark our Exodus. We were told to roast

---

lips' (*Shemos*, 6:30). This suggests that he would have a hard time pronouncing letters rooted in the lips, such as P (Pei) or B (Beis), etc. Yet, the essential letters in *Pakod Yifkod* are the two Pei's (see also *Yalkut Shimoni*, 64). The fact that Moshe was able to pronounce these words, and do so clearly, as if "the Shechinah was speaking through him," confirmed his legitimacy as the Redeemer.

the lamb over a spit — and the lamb should be with "its head upon its legs" (*Shemos*, 12:9). As the Tzemach Tzedek (third Chabad Rebbe) explains (*Derech Mitzvosechah*, Korban Pesach), this is the fetal position of a child in the womb, ready to be born.

Today, when we no longer offer a Paschal Lamb we place an egg on the Seder plate to commemorate an offering that was performed in the Temple. Although this is not to memorialize the Paschal Lamb, rather the *Chagigah* offering, it still shares the above symbolism. An egg is where a young chick resides in a fetal state, symbolizing the pregnancy of a new reality.

An embryo and even a fetus is not yet a full individual — it is still an extension of the mother. In the words of the sage Rabbi Eliezer, "*Ubar Yerech Imo* / a fetus is no more than a thigh of its mother" (*Chulin*, 58a). In Egypt, the Israelites were not yet realized as a People; they were still in the fetal state of possibility. All that a fetus, so to speak, can do is hope and dream to be born. Yet, this 'dream state' was also the beginning of their new collective existence.

In this tenuous stage of pure potential prior to the full formation of the child, it is important that the parents visualize positive imagery and outcomes towards the process of birth. This is also true at the moment of conception. What the parents think and perceive during conception can have a spiritual and even physically formative influence on the child. The Medrash mentions a story (which can be debated whether it is literal or figurative) of a dark skinned Gentile king and dark skinned Gentile queen who gave birth to a lighter skinned child. Rabbi Akiva suggested that at the time of conception the queen was gazing upon a light colored statue, which thus impacted the skin color of the child born from this union (*Tanchumah*, Naso).

The Ramban speaks at length about the power of vision, especially at the time of conception. According to him we should be surrounded by holy images at that time (*Igeres Kodesh*). In the Torah we read about Ya'akov and his father-in-law Lavan, and the story of how Ya'akov managed to get all the spotted and striped sheep. Ya'akov employed imagistic cues during the animals' mating process to affect the appearance of their offspring. "And Ya'akov took rods from fresh-cut branches…and made white stripes on them by peeling the bark and exposing the white inner wood of the branches…. Then he placed the peeled branches in all the watering troughs, so that they would be directly in front of the flocks when they came to drink, and they should conceive when they drank. And the flocks conceived in front of the rods, and they bore young that were streaked or speckled or spotted" (*Bereishis*, 30:37-39). By looking at striped rods at the time of conception, the white sheep were influenced to have offspring that were striped. The white wood in front of the darker surface of the watering troughs served to magnify the contrast, and the clear water itself served to amplify this perception.

The imagination and visualizations of the mother particularly affect the child, both spiritually and physically. Once pregnancy commences, stress and gene markers can be turned on or kept dormant depending on what the pregnant woman chooses to eat, for example, and her mood during the pregnancy. Throughout Iyyar we are each pregnant with the potential of revelation and must take our 'labor' seriously. The daily meditation on the *Sefiros* is a wonderful opportunity to cultivate positive visualizations of our future selves, our people, and the world to come.

In any case, the pregnancy and fetal development of *Klal Yisrael* / the People of Israel in Egypt was extremely influential in relation to who we were to become, whether from the perspective of the pregnant mother or the developing child. Our tenacious faith allowed us to visualize the possibility of freedom even under the most degrading conditions of subjugation. Our positive imagination gave us the courage and resiliency to take the taboo animal of our enslavers and offer it as a *Korban* to Hashem. These formative 'in-utero' experiences became ingrained in our people's DNA, and formed the foundation of our collective existence even until today.

Labor prior to Birth

Going out of Egypt is the birth of Klal Yisrael, and the plagues that preceded the exodus are the pains of childbirth. The plagues in Egypt and at the Sea parallel the process of childbirth. The plagues of blood, loud frogs, wild animals, for example, says the Arizal, parallel, the blood, the wailing, and wild involuntary reactions during childbirth. All the plagues are part of the contractions and birth pangs that expelled Klal Yisrael from the womb. The departure from Egypt was the beginning of labor; and the splitting of the sea, together with our passing through it, was the delivery.

When a child is born he opens his mouth and gives a loud cry. As we were born as a People, and crossed the split sea, we opened our mouths and began to sing the *Shirah*, the 'Song of the Sea.' Similarly, from the perspective of a laboring mother, we rejoiced in the birth of Klal Yisrael, our hidden potential revealed.

Birth and Tumah

While birth, and bringing forth new life, is a tremendously joyous event, for the mother it can also be laced with a sense of loss and sadness. A measure of grief or 'post-partum depression' sets in following the birth. One reason for this is that the baby has been attached to the mother in an intimate oneness. Now the baby is forcefully pushed or perhaps pulled out of her body, and separated from this beautiful, albeit perhaps very uncomfortable, state of oneness. Recognizing the weight of this physical, emotional, and spiritual separation, the Torah established this time as a period of *Tumah*, a 'post-birth Niddah.' This is a form of mourning for the mother, as she has lost a piece of herself, so to speak (Ba'al HaTurim, Tazria). During this time, therefore, the wife is 'closed' to physical intimacy, and remains separate from her spouse.

A new baby, a third person with many needs, has been placed into the equation of the marriage. The parents, who have been connected as lovers and spouses, must now learn to connect on another level as well, as collaborators in the raising of a child. Deeply focused on their baby, the parents can seemingly stop being interested in each other. They can forget that they are also spouses. A happy spousal relationship is integral to a happy home and a happy child. It also makes it possible for the parents to have more children. Therefore, the post-birth Niddah, like the monthly Niddah, serves to awaken desire between the couple to reunite. They are given time to process post-birth feelings, and to be totally preoccupied with the baby. Thus the post-birth Niddah period is longer than the more regular monthly Niddah, as the psycho-physical situation requires.

In the narrative of the Exodus and our birth at the sea, we become a people with many needs. With this dramatic new status, it is possible to forget the deeper purpose of our Exodus and our intimate relationship with Hashem. We can become preoccupied with being a people, and forget our Divine Spouse, as it were. Therefore, we count a period of seven weeks, and spend the month of Iyyar arousing our desire to be in close personal relationship with Hashem. Hashem basically tells us, 'I will give you the Torah, but just not yet — I want you to wait so that you will deeply want it, and desire to receive it from Me.'

This existential separation arouses our spiritual longing and desire.

A Time of Bedikah / Checking, Examining

Both pre-birth Niddah and post-birth Niddah have to do with blood, a loss of life-force, and a need to regenerate the potential to give life. The post-birth Niddah ensues at the moment of birth, even if theoretically there is no blood. In both scenarios, at the end of the 'red' days of bleeding or birthing, there begin seven 'clean' or 'white' days. White alludes to the lack of blood stains, and to the custom of wearing white undergarments.*

---

* Perhaps a connection can be made with the Torah archetype of *Lavan* / Laban whose name means 'white.' The Arizal writes that until Lag b'Omer we are under the influence of

The seven weeks of the Omer period thus represent the seven clean or 'white' days leading up to the expansive union of Shavuos.

On each of these 'seven clean days' a woman performs a *Bedikah* /internal examination, to confirm that there is no more flow of menstrual blood. Inwardly, Bedikah represents a time of self-inspection and introspection. During the seven weeks of the Omer we also perform a daily Bedikah, a self-examination, carefully confirming the 'purity' of our emotional and developmental states, as symbolized by the *Midos* which we meditate on every day. In fact, it is taught that the counting and the accompanying Bedikah itself, during this time, have the power to *create* that state of purity necessary to receive the Torah (*Zohar* 3, 97a. As some Poskim teach, the Bedikah of the Niddah itself establishes a form of *Taharah* / 'purity' *Chazon Ish*, Yoreh Deah, 80:20). We therefore see that our active participation is needed in the process of our own purification. This realization is both an empowering opportunity as well as a serious responsibility.

Lavan, and from Lag b'Omer on we are not under his influence (*Sha'ar HaKavanos*, Sefiras haOmer, Derush 12). When Lavan chased Ya'akov, his son in law, who ran away from him in fear of being cheated, together the two decided, "...Let us form a covenant, you and I, and may He be a witness between me and you. Ya'akov took a stone and set it up [as] a monument... (And Lavan said) 'This pile is a witness, and this monument is a witness, that I will not pass this pile [to go] to you and that you shall not pass this pile and this monument to [come to] me to [do] harm'" (*Bereishis*, 31:44-52). The words the Torah uses is "This pile is a witness...I will not pass this pile." 'Pile' in Hebrew is *Gal*, so Lavan is saying, 'The *Gal* is the witness, the barrier, that I cannot pass over.' *Gal* is *Lag* backwards, so the *Gal*, the pile, alludes to Lag b'Omer. Thus Lavan the oppressor does not pass the 33rd day. For the majority of the Omer we are under the influence of Lavan. Since Lavan literally means 'white,' we can see this as an allusion to the idea of the 'white days,' the days of waiting in separation and Katnus for the upcoming return to unity and Gadlus.

Each day of the seven weeks we examine and inspect another aspect of our emotions along with its outward expression. We probe and examine ourselves to ensure that there is an internal sense of balance and harmony on an emotional level, so that when we reunite with Hashem and receive the Torah, we will be an open, prepared vessel, properly equipped to absorb and integrate what is offered to us.

Matan Torah / the Giving of the Torah represents the revealed unity between a husband and wife (*Ta'anis*, 26b), the re-unification that comes after a period of separation and longing (see *Rashi*, "Zeh Matan Torah, ibid). When this unification occurs following the separation it is much more powerful and more deeply felt than before the separation. In the end, it is revealed that the status of ultimate unity had withstood the circumstance of separation, and actually grew stronger as a result of it.

Lag b'Omer:
The Peak of Separation and Paradoxical Unity

Now we can understand another deep dimension of Lag b'Omer. Insofar as the 49 days of the Omer are a time of Katnus, Din, Tumah, separation, longing, and desire; what then is the role of Lag B'Omer? Why do we celebrate? As we said previously, we celebrate because on Lag B'Omer, the 33rd day of the Omer, the supermajority of the 49 days have passed and are behind us (*Maharsha, Moed Katan*, 28a). On the other hand, the supermajority should also represent the peak of the Omer, expressing the full potency of its Katnus, Din, Tumah, and separation. From this vantage point, Lag b'Omer is the time of greatest separation. However, the paradox is this: when there is a deep separation it arouses and awakens an even deeper longing to be together. The greater the outward separation of two that belong together, the greater the inward longing and the pull towards each other. Externally, Lag b'Omer may appear to represent the height of separation, but inwardly it is the depths of longing; powerful longing reveals the deepest connection. Thus, Lag b'Omer reveals an indelible *Yichud* / unity, not only *despite* the peak of separation, but precisely *because* of it.

This also helps to explain a grammatical anomaly. The phrase *Lag b'Omer* literally means the 33rd day "*in*" the counting of the Omer. Grammatically, it would be more correct to call it Lag *l'Omer* — the 33rd day "from" the (beginning of the) Omer. Some Sefardim do in fact call this day *Lag l'Omer*, yet the most common custom is to call it Lag *b'*Omer. Why?

Lag b'Omer is in fact a celebrational day "*in*" the Omer; meaning that it is completely rooted within the dynamic of the Omer. Lag b'Omer thus embodies and amplifies the inner quality, the quintessence of the Omer. As we have learned, the Omer period is generally a time of harsh Din and separation; that is the external manifestation of the energy of the Omer. However, the inner essence of this Din and separation — namely intense longing and hidden unity — is especially revealed on Lag b'Omer.[*]

There is the "crown of Torah" and the "crown of priesthood" (*Avos*, 4:13). Moshe received the crown of Torah, Aaron the crown of priesthood.

---

[*] An allusion to this idea of Lag b'Omer as the day that truly embodies the essential energy of the Omer, is reflected in the fact that the Omer offering, besides what was actually

There are 24 books of Tanach / full written Torah, and there are 24 gifts that were given to the Kohanim. Taken together, the 24 books of Tanach and the 24 gifts of the Kohanim total forty-eight, corresponding to the 48 days between going out of Egypt and properly preparing to receive the Torah, which leads to us eventually becoming a 'nation of priests.'

The first 24 days are connected to Moshe, and the next 24 days are Aaron's. Chazal list all the 24 gifts of Moshe,* followed by the 24 gifts of Aaron (*Chulin*, 133b, Rashi ad loc). The 9th gift of Aaron is the Omer. The 9th gift of Aaron corresponds to the 33rd day in this order; which is especially significant considering that the 9th gift is the Mitzvah of Counting the Omer. We see from this that Lag b'Omer, the 33rd, symbolically embodies the entire Omer period.

That is why the 'death' of Rashbi is celebrated as opposed to mourned. On Lag b'Omer we are focusing on the inner essence of the Omer. Death is only a separation on the physical level, of the body from the soul. However, the external separation brings about / reveals a deeper inseparability. In the words of the Zohar, "When a Tzadik departs he is to be found in all the worlds, even more than during his lifetime" (*Zohar* 3, 71b. *Tanya*, Iggeres HaKodesh, 27). Lag

---

offered on the altar, is distributed to the Kohanim (priests), and through the Kohanim it is connected to the number 33.

* The numerical value of the word *Purim* (336) equals that of Aharon haKohen, and the numerical value of the word Lag b'Omer equals the name Moshe = 345. Interestingly, the same day of the week Purim falls out on will be the same day in the week for Lag b'Omer, so if Purim is on Sunday Lag b'Omer will be on Sunday. Both Purim and Lag b'Omer are connected with the assimilation of Torah. On Purim there was a full acceptance of the (revealed) Torah (*Shabbos*, 88a). And on Lag b'Omer there was the revealing of the hidden aspects of Torah, through Rashbi, who was also a 'spark' of Moshe.

b'Omer is a celebration of the *Penimiyus* / internal, secret dimension of life. Thus, precisely on the day of his 'death,' Rashbi reveals the greatest teachings of the internal Torah, the deepest truth of eternal life and ultimate unification.

This is *Chai Iyyar*, the *Chayus* of Iyyar, the life-force in longing. On one level, it is the day of Rashbi's death, and on another level it is the day he was born (literally and figuratively); the day he left the 'womb' of the cave and began to reveal that which can never die.

The Matan Torah of Inner Torah

Lag b'Omer is always the same day of the week as Purim. On Purim we fully received the Torah (*Shabbos* 88a), and more specifically, the 'Oral Torah' after the exile — less than 100 years after the *Churban* / destruction of the First Beis haMikdash (*P'nei Yehoshua*, ad loc. *Tanchumah*, Noach, 3). On Lag b'Omer we received the 'inner aspect of the Oral Torah' — less than 100 years from the *Churban* of the Second Beis haMikdash.

The giving of the 'outer' Torah, the Written Torah, occurs in Sivan, when we arrive at Mount Sinai. The giving of the 'inner' aspect of the Oral Torah occurs in the height of Iyyar, before we arrive at Mount Sinai. From an internal perspective, an 'arriving' can happen even in the state of 'not yet arriving.' In other words, there can be unity even in separation. Indeed, from a *Penimiyus* perspective — the greater the external separation, the greater the internal connection.

The revealing of the inner Torah is the revealing of the *Ohr ha-Ganuz* / Hidden Light, a Divine light that appears outwardly as darkness. Why is the *Ohr haGanuz* revealed specifically on the 33rd day of the Omer?

The 33rd word in the *Chumash* / Five Books of Moshe is *Tov* / goodness (*Bereishis*, 1:4). As we already know, the number 33 is written in Hebrew as the letters Lamed-Gimel. These letters in reverse order are Gimmel-Lamed, spelling *Gal* / reveal. One of the inner meanings of *Lag* is therefore 'a revealing of goodness.'

The previous day, day 32, is *Lamed Beis*, spelling the word *Lev* / heart. After our 32 days of hard work and harsh Din, we can now proceed to 'reveal' the 'goodness' within the very 'heart' of the Omer period. Put another way, the good heart hidden in the harshness of the Omer period is revealed on Lag b'Omer. Also, the yearning of our hearts for Hashem in hard times reveals Hashem's ever-present goodness.[*]

The Hidden Light

When the Torah mentions 'Tov,' the 33rd word, it is referring to the light of the first day — declaring that the light was good: "Hashem saw the *Ohr* / light and it was *Tov* / good." What is this primordial light the Torah refers to? It is certainly not sunlight, as the sun is only created, or only begins to function, on the Fourth

---

[*] Rashbi is of the opinion (*Sifra*, Bachukosai, 2:1-2) that the ultimate Messianic transformation of "wild, predatory animals" (literally and figuratively), is not that they are eradicated, rather, that they exist and are gentle. Meaning, that they reveal the inner 'goodness' within them.

Day of Creation. It is a supernal light, the *Ohr haGanuz* / hidden light, which reveals everything. Looking with that light one can see from one end of the world to the next. This is the light of unity.

When Moshe sees a light in the thorn bush, he sees that it is a fire but that the fire is not consuming the bush. The thorn bush remains intact. This is the light of unity that does not destroy other things in order to exist. It is like a blazing fire that paradoxically allows even a dry thorn bush to remain undisturbed.

Note that the word *Ohr* / light appears five times in the beginning of *Bereishis* / Genesis, and the word *Sneh* / thorn bush appears five times in the beginning of *Shemos* / Exodus. This is a hint that the light revealed in the first book of the Torah, the *Ohr haGanuz*, is the very same light that is revealed to Moshe at the burning bush.

How can we access this hidden light? Where was it hidden? According to the Baal Shem Tov, it was hidden within the Torah. Thus the *Tov*, the "it was good" of the light, refers to the higher light of Torah, which is the hidden source of all goodness. After the first 32 days of the Omer have passed there are 17 days left; Lag b'Omer is 17 days before the giving of the Torah on the Sixth of Sivan. The number 17 is the value of the word *Tov* / good. Thus, Lag b'Omer is the beginning of the revelation of the *Tov*, the good light that was hidden within the Torah, the same light that was hidden at the beginning of Creation.

The first 32 days of the Omer is when most of the hard work of this period takes place. To put it more poetically, the hardest *avodah* / work of the Omer is the *Avodas haLev* / the work of the heart — the first *Lev* / 32 days. Once we pass the *Lev* days we can more easily be open to the *Tov* / 17 days, the pure goodness of life.* However, eventually we realize that this goodness, the *Ohr HaGanuz,* was really there the whole time, we just were not able to see it. By embracing Katnus in a time of Din, we discover that Gadlus is always hidden in the here and now.

The Hidden aspects of the Torah's inner light have been here since the first day of creation. Redemption is always secretly concealed within exile. Rashbi and Lag b'Omer both together reveal the *Sod / secret* of the Torah, the hidden internal Gadlus, in order to bring about our ultimate Redemption within the revealed, external world.

This inner light of the Torah is a light that illuminates our exile and darkness with the glow of goodness. At the burning bush, Hashem spoke through the miraculous fire to announce the imminent Redemption. Thus is it the inner light of the Torah that beckons us and brings us out of exile. It is the Torah of Moshiach. This light reveals the true 'face of Reality,' the inner essence, and hidden goodness within all judgments, exiles, and darkness. It shines precisely from within where the darkness had been. It is the light that shines into our exile and thus the light that brings us out of our exile.

All of the above explorations related to separation and unification, death and life, mourning and celebration, exile and redemption, hiddenness and revelation, fit well with the major reasons given for celebrating Lag b'Omer:

---

* Torah is received on the 50th day, corresponding to the 50 Gates of Binah. During the first 32 days, we are receiving the 32 paths of Chochmah. Once the 33rd day ensues we are more connected with the 50 gates of Binah. Binah is connected with joy (*Eim haBanim Semeicha* / a joyful mother of children) and thus there is more joy after the first 32 days of the Omer.

The students stopped dying on the 33rd of the Omer. The time of Din and Katnus has passed and Gadlus is beginning to be revealed more openly. The inner Torah starts to be revealed as a prelude to Shavuos.

It is the day that Rashbi leaves the cave and becomes the paragon of contemplative, inner Torah teachings, beginning with the Zohar. These are the teachings that will stimulate Redemption from exile.

It is the day Rashbi reveals the *Idra* before he dies. As the deepest part of the inner Torah, this reveals the hidden light, the *Tov*, of the future redeemed world, here and now.

The Inner and Outer Weddings

As we have begun to explain, Shavuos is the *Matan Torah* / receiving of the Revealed Torah, and Lag b'Omer is known as the Matan Torah of *Penimiyus haTorah* / inner Torah. These two days are thus deeply interlinked. The numerical value of the words *Lag* (33) and *b'Omer* (312) equal 345, the same value as the name Moshe, who is the great revealer of Torah on Shavuos. According to the Arizal, Rashbi is in fact the *Gilgul* / reincarnation of Moshe (There are many other parallels between Moshe and Rashbi: see *Hilula D'Rashbi* (Margoliyus), Moshe Rabbeinu v'Rashbi. "You (Moshe) ascended on high, you took *Shevi* /captives" (*Tehilim*, 68:19. *Shabbos*, 89a). What is Shevi? The acronym for **Sh**imon **B**ar **Y**ochai. Moshe became impregnated with the soul of the Rashbi (*Semichas Chachamim* (Katz), Hakdamah, p. 140). Additionally, the day of Lag b'Omer always falls out on the same day of the week as the fourth day of Sukkos, the day that we welcome the *Ushpiz* / archetypal guest Moshe.

Shavuos, the Giving of the Torah, is called 'the cosmic wedding day.' *Yom Chasunoso zu Matan Torah* / the day of His wedding is the day we received the Torah. The day that Rashbi passes away from this world is similarly called a *Hilulah*, one meaning of which is also a wedding. But on the surface this seems very puzzling; how is death like a wedding? And how can we receive an aspect of Torah in a time of separation, i.e. death? A wedding reveals the unity of apparent opposites, while death is a separation of previously unified elements.

As the cosmic wedding, Shavuos reveals the unity between our will and Hashem's Will, between the finite and the Infinite, between the 'feminine' Shechinah (of which we are 'limbs') and *Kudsha Berich Hu* — the 'masculine' Transcendent One.

For seven weeks following Her 'post-birth Niddah cycle,' the Shechinah remains separate from her Mate. After this extended period of yearning, cleansing, and preparing, She is finally unified with the Transcendent One in a great wedding outwardly manifest as the giving of the Torah.

This narrative of alternating periods of separation and unification, romantic as it is, comes from a *Nigleh* / revealed or outer perspective. From this perspective, a time of separation excludes unification. At the deepest point of this separation, however, when two thirds of the days of her separation are complete, there is an inner wedding, an inner unification of some kind. How is this so?

As mentioned, everything has an outer and an inner dynamic. From an outer perspective we need to wait the full seven weeks for the wedding; diligently checking ourselves each day to ensure our purity. From an inner perspective, however, the greater yearning, longing, and desire to connect that we experience in separation actually reveals a deeper unity that is already present even before the outer wedding. At the peak of the separation there is the greatest yearning for unity. Thus, inwardly, the longing itself *is* an expression of the deepest unity.

The ultimate reason the *Penimiyus haTorah* / inner aspect of the Torah is revealed on Lag b'Omer is because Lag b'Omer is the supermajority, the peak of the Omer, the peak of the yearning for Matan Torah. Lag b'Omer is the peak of the yearning of the Shechina for Her Beloved. In the last third of the Omer there is a *Reshimu* / imprint or reflection shining backwards in time from Shavuos. The sunlight of the *Nigleh* / Revealed Torah of Shavuos is reflected in Lag b'Omer's revelation, like the light of the moon as it bursts over the horizon.

There are two ways to reveal unity: a) overtly, as when two people who love each other deeply are physically together, and b) covertly, as when they are *Davka* / specifically furthest apart and longing for each other the most. This is the deepest level of *Yichud* / unity hidden within apparent *Pirud* / separation.

Shavuos reveals overt unity; we finally arrive at the *Chuppah* / wedding canopy. The Inner Torah of Lag b'Omer reveals hidden unity, unity in separation; we arrive without arriving. Penimiyus haTorah is thus the remedy for exile (a.k.a. night, the state of not having arrived). Rashbi represents the teaching that even in exile, there is home - in being lost, there is a finding.

Rashbi and Lag b'Omer are both representative of the revelation that in the depth of separation there is a greater longing, and thus a greater connection. Among the twelve tribes of Israel, the tribe of Shimon, the original namesake of Rashbi, is most connected to this type of quality and awareness. Among other things this type of awareness imbues one with a more subtle understanding of the nature of a 'sinner,' someone who is distant and has separated himself from the Source of All Life; and specifically how it is precisely this person who has the ability to reach the greatest spiritual heights.

The tribe (and the son of Ya'akov) Shimon is related to the level of *Sod* / secret, the hiddenness connected to the place of *Safek* / doubt, the place of uncertainty (*Mei haShiloach*, Toldos). For instance, when Ya'akov is giving his *Bracha* / prophetic blessing to Shimon, he says Shimon has a "secret" (*Bereishis*, 49:6). The secret is that Shimon listens — he empathizes fully with people and connects with their places of doubt — the places where they doubt if they are loveable, the places where they stumble into mistakes and depravity. In fact, the name *Shimon* has the letters of the words *Sham Aven* / there is depravity there (*Toldos Aaron*, (Zelichav) Pinchas), alluding to his ability to listen to the darkest doubts within people. Shimon was the defender of his sister Dinah after she was violated. Generations later, a head of the tribe of Shimon, Zimri, became the defender of the 'sinners' of Klal Yisrael in the episode of the idolatry of Ba'al Peor. In this way, Shimon represents the hidden way, the way of the Ba'al Teshuvah, the embrace of all people, no matter their current state or status.

According to the *Ra'avad* (*Pirush on Sefer Yetzirah*; see also *Yalkut Reuveini*, Vayeshev), the order of the months follows the order of Ya'akov's sons as recounted in the book of *Shemos* when it lists the names of the people who went down to Egypt. To quote, "These are the names of the sons of Ya'akov who went to Egypt… *Reuvein, Shimon, Levi,* and *Yehudah…*" (*Shemos*, 1:1-5). According to this *Seder* / order, the tribe associated with the month of Iyyar is Shimon, and Shimon, by name, is connected to Rashbi, Rabbi Shimon bar Yochai. In fact, there is a mystical, 'hidden' tradition that the Rashbi is not only named Shimon, but moreover, that he is from the tribe of Shimon (*Mei haShiloach*, Tetzavah. R. Tzadok, *Takanans HaShavim*, 6). And thus, as the Karliner Rebbe said, "Just as Hashem is G-d to all people, the same is with Rashbi, he is for all people, even sinners" (*Beis Aaron*, 106b). Indeed, Rashbi is particularly connected to the revelation that in the depth of separation and 'sin' there is a greater longing, a deeper connection, and thus a greater potential for a more illuminating revelation of light.

CONCLUSION

Rabbi Akiva at first *fought* the exile, and backed the Bar Kochva revolt. He suggested that we fight fire with fire. Following the crushing defeat of Bar Kochva, Rashbi — one of his five remaining students — responded differently. Rashbi's response to the tragedy was that: exile is not to be fought, but rather *illuminated*. Thus he revealed the Zohar, which literally means to 'shine,' the Hidden Light of *Geulah* / Redemption. In this light we are able to glimpse the greatest secret; exile is not actually separate from Redemption. The light of the moon *is* the light of the sun.

When outwardly we reach the end of our thousands of years in exile, and celebrate our final and eternal wedding with the Transcendent One, *biM'heira b'Yamienu* / may this be speedily, in our days, we will then cry out: "Thank you Hashem for hiding from me all this time! *Odcha Hashem ki Anafta Bi* / Thank you Hashem for appearing to be angry with me all those years" (*Yeshayah* 12:1).

"My soul thirsts for You, my flesh longs for You (as) in a dry and weary land without water! So may I look for You in the sanctuary to see Your power and Your glory" (*Tehilim.* 63:2-3). According to the Baal Shem Tov, the phrase "so may I look for you," means *Halevai* / if only. '*If only* we will be as thirsty for You when we finally arrive (and can physically see Your glory in the sanctuary), as we were when we felt distant, alienated, and rejected in the wilderness of the world.' Exile has given us something we could not have attained any other way: a soul that mightily thirsts for her Beloved. This deep spiritual thirst expresses a very deep connection that is revealed specifically because of such longing, yearning, and desiring to be close to Hashem. This is the light hidden within darkness, the life within death, the inner Torah of Lag b'Omer revealed by Rashbi.

Chapter Two

CUSTOMS & PRACTICES OF LAG B'OMER

1) Bonfires

2) Meron: Grave of Rashbi

3) Bows & Arrows

4) Parades

5) Upsherin

6) Zohar, Songs in Honor of Rashbi

BONFIRES

One of the most well-known customs of Lag b'Omer is to light a bonfire. The simple reason to light bonfires is to gather people in celebration (*Gittin*, 57a). A letter written in 1489 CE by the famous Italian sage Rabbi Ovadiah Bartenura mentions people making a trek to Meron, Israel, the burial site of Rashbi, to pray and light celebratory bonfires. Additionally, we know the holy Ohr HaChayim, Rabbi Chayim ben Attar (1696-1743), participated and even offered some material to the bonfire that was lit in honor of the Rashbi on Lag b'Omer (see, *Kevod Malachim*, at the end).

Arguably, this practice is perhaps an artifact related to the rebellion during the life of the Rashbi, as the Jewish rebels would have made campfires during their military excursions. Yet, every custom has both a historical reason and a meta-historical intention, a physical logic and a spiritual motivation. *Chazal* / Sages are not interested in history per se, rather, in meta-history. In other words, Chazal are not as interested in what happened physically as they are in what spiritually *caused* it to happen, and what we can learn from those events. Chazal do not (openly) associate Lag b'Omer and the Omer period with anything connected to Bar Kochva (The Lubavitcher Rebbe, *Igros Kodesh* 9, p. 64), and so, it behooves us to go a little deeper and connect the bonfires themselves with the *Penimiyus* / internal reality of Lag b'Omer and the life and teachings of the Rashbi. We need, therefore, to explore the connection between bonfires and the inner Torah.

On the day of a person's *Yahrtzeit* / anniversary of passing there is a custom of lighting a candle to honor their memory (*Maharshal*, Siman 46. *Magen Avraham*, 261:6). While there is no apparent source for this practice in Medrash or Gemara, it has nonetheless been widely accepted and passed down as a worthwhile and relevant custom. According to Rabbeinu Bachya, the early 14th Century commentator, "The soul is delighted by the lighting of candles. She expands from the pleasure she receives from the light." In other words, lighting a flame for the soul that has left the world not only gives them honor, but also benefit and pleasure.

Our soul itself is our guiding light, like a flame, and the soul's light can illuminate the darkness of the world, "A candle of Hashem is the soul of man" (*Mishlei*, 20:27. *Shabbos* 32a). When we light a candle for someone who passes, in a sense, it makes the light of their soul visible. Light is connected to Tzadikim; *Ohr Tzadikim Yismach* / the light of the Tzadikim will bring joy (*Mishlei*, 13:9). Since the Tzadik Rashbi's soul is so brilliant, a single candle does not suffice, we need to light many lights. Those lights combine, as it were, to form a bonfire.

Rashbi was such a great Tzadik that he is credited as confirming that, "...the Torah will never be forgotten" (*Shabbos*, 138b).* The word *Shichecha* / forgetfulness has the same letters and is connected in meaning to the word *Choshech* / darkness. Rashbi ensures us that Divine Light will prevail in the world, even in exile, rather than darkness and forgetfulness. Rashbi left the world with the gift of the inner teachings of Torah, revealed in *Sefer haZohar* / the Book of Illumination. Therefore, we light fires to illuminate the darkness of night, literally and metaphorically.

The *Sod* / secret teachings of Torah are conceptually connected with fire. In the Gemara, when Rabbi Eleazar Ben Arach was teaching Sod, "a fire descended" from Heaven and encompassed all the trees in the field (*Chagigah*, 14b). Similarly, when Rabbi Yonason Ben Uziel taught Sod, a fire manifested that burned the birds flying over his head (*Sukkah*, 28a). However, when Hillel the Elder, the greatest sage amongst these (as well as the teacher of R. Yonason Ben Uziel) taught Sod, nothing is recorded to have happened; perhaps, because when Hillel taught Torah, the fire manifested that did not consume anything. This is a higher level of fire, the *Ohr haGanuz* / hidden light of the first day that also appeared to Moshe at the burning bush.

---

* In general, in most areas in Halacha, we do not rule as the Rashbi (*Eiruvin*, 46b. see also, *Teshuvas Maharshal*, Siman 98). Yet, in areas of the hidden Torah, the secrets of the Torah, we do rule as the Rashbi. When Rabbi Shimon declares, "The Torah will never be forgotten from Israel," this is an undisputed statement. For here, Rashbi is talking about Klal Yisrael as a whole, and the secret of their eternity.

Fire and the Ohr haGanuz

As we have explored at length in Part Two, the 33rd day of the Omer is related to the 33rd word in the Torah, which is *Tov* / good. *Tov* is Hashem's description of *Ohr* / Light created on the First Day: "Hashem saw the light and it was good" (*Bereishis*, 1:4). This primordial light, created before the sun and moon, was hidden from view (*Chagigah*, 12a). Thus it is called *Ohr haGanuz* / the Hidden Light — and the Baal Shem Tov teaches that this Primordial Light was hidden within the Torah (*Degel Machana Ephrayim*, Bereishis. *Yosher Divrei Emes*, 3. See *Zohar* 1, p, 264a).

The Torah has "two lights," the light of the revealed aspects of Torah and the light of the hidden aspects of Torah. Lag b'Omer is *Tov* / 17 days before Shavuos, the revealing of the external aspects of Torah. Lag b'Omer itself was the revealing of the internal aspects of Torah. In celebration of these multiple lights of the Torah, we light a fire containing multiple flames.

The day that Rashbi passed away, he revealed the deepest teachings of the Zohar. As witnessed by the Zohar itself, a fantastic light filled the world with this revelation (*Idra Zuta*, Zohar 3). A great spiritual fire also surrounded the home of Rashbi, preventing anyone from getting close to Rashbi besides his closest students. This light was revealed to everyone present, even following his demise, until the evening, when they were able to approach his body and bury him. We therefore light a bonfire to reenact the revelation of such a magnificent light on this awesome day — a revelation that continues to shine in our own times as well.

There are different kinds of fire, including a) the simple, gentle flame of a single wick, and b) the blistering flames of a torch or bonfire. The basic difference between these two is that the wick is singular and the torch and bonfire are comprised of many wicks, sticks, or logs. A simple candle represents Shabbos — simple oneness, rest and Redemption. A torch represents weekdays — separation, complication, effort, and exile.

Before Shabbos begins, to welcome the rest and oneness of Shabbos, we light candles with one wick each. When Shabbos ends, as we enter the work week, we light a Havdalah candle, which is a torch, with multiple wicks unified together. This more concentrated fire shines brightly to give us the strength for the ensuing efforts of the week. This torch represents the Torah that comes down into exile and lifts us out. The concentrated light of Rashbi's Torah gives us the strength not only to survive exile, but to lift ourselves out of it, and to create unity out of the separation, to create one great flame from 'many wicks.' This bonfire thus represents the hidden aspects of Torah that are designed to light up our life, even in the darkness of exile.

MERON:
THE GRAVE OF RASHBI

Rabbi Ovadia Bartenura, in a letter to his brother from the year 1489 CE, writes that when people would come on the 18th day of Iyyar* to the grave of Rashbi and light great bonfires, many barren women and sick people were healed in connection to the *Tzedaka* / charity they gave there. A short time later, in the 1500's, we find that the Arizal went up to the grave of Rashbi on Lag b'Omer and stayed there for three days. Rabbi Chayim Vital writes that he did this "according to the custom of Israel." This clearly suggests that this was a very established custom before the times of the Arizal.**

---

* Perhaps a correct version of the letter would say the 28th of Iyyar rather than the 18th. The 28th of Iyyar marks the death of Shemuel the Prophet.

** Regarding the Arizal going up to Meron on Lag b'Omer, and it being a day of joy, see *Sha'ar haKavanos*, Inyan Pesach, Derush 12; *Sha'ar Sefiros haOmer*, 7; *Magen Avraham*, Orach Chayim, Siman 493:3; *Ateres Zekeinim, Ibid*. The Chasam Sofer opposed making Lag b'Omer a day of joy and celebration, since it is a "new holiday" (*Chasam Sofer* on Yoreh Deah, Siman 233). Others were opposed to bonfires and the burning of clothes (a practice

A relatively modern custom is to donate *Chai Rotel / 18 Rotels* or measures of drink (a *Rotel* is a liquid measure of about 3 liters; 18 Rotels equals 54 liters), or the monetary equivalent, to those who have made the trip to pray at the gravesite of Rashbi on Lag b'Omer.

If is not possible for one to make the pilgrimage to Meron, many substitute visiting *Kivrei Tzadikim* / Gravesites of Tzadikim elsewhere. Many in Israel have the custom to pray on Lag b'Omer at the grave of Shimon haTzadik, the tomb of the *Kohen Gadol* / High Priest during the 5th Century BCE. This idea extends as well to the gravesites of all Tzadikim, as the "the sand of the earth is one," and thus all burial sites of Tzadikim are interconnected (*Kav Hayashar*). Visiting the grave of any Tzadik is a good practice on Lag b'Omer.

☾

---

of Lag b'Omer), and in general making a celebration when we are remembering the death of a Tzadik (R. Yosef Shaul Nathanson, *Shoel u'Meishiv.* 5. Siman 39. "Any connection to death that involves burning of vessels (not simply, regarding a king's garments or belongings, *Avodah Zarah*, 11a. *Yirmiyahu* 34:5. *Yorah De'ah*, Siman 348:1)…know that this is connected to idol worship" Rambam, *Hilchos Aku'm*, 9:5). Yet, *Minhag Yisrael Torah Hu* / a custom of Israel is Torah. The very universal acceptance of these customs itself is their validation. Ben Ish Chai, *Torah l'Shma*, 400. See at length R Shmuel Helel, *Kevod Malachim*. Burning clothes reminds us of Adam and Chava who were, before eating from the Tree of Knowledge, without garments. Rashbi reached that level as well, sitting without garments in the cave (*Shabbos*, 33b), thus, symbolically, on Lag b'Omer garments are burned (see R. Yehoshua of Kutna, *Yeshuos Malko*, p. 152).

BOW & ARROW

On Lag b'Omer there is a custom to go out into the fields and play with a toy bow and arrow. While this is mostly done by children, many great sages and Tzadikim have, and still do, symbolically shoot arrows on Lag b'Omer.

A bow is simply a reminder of the rainbow, says the B'nei Yissaschar (Chodesh Iyyar, 3:4). It is interesting to note that in Hebrew, as well as English, both objects have the same name, 'bow' and 'rainbow,' and in Hebrew both are called *Keshes*. The rainbow, the Torah tells us, is a symbol of the covenant between Hashem and humanity that the world will not be destroyed even if we become as corrupt as the generation that warranted the Great Flood. Of course, a rainbow is a natural phenomenon, nevertheless it is there to remind us of a supernatural covenant. During the life of Rashbi, says the Gemara, there was never a rainbow (Yerushalmi, *Berachos* 9:2).

What does this mean?

Firstly, Rashbi himself is associated with the rainbow. The word *haKeshes* is numerically 805: Hei/5 + Kuf/100 + Shin/300 + Tav/400 = 805. This is the same value as the full name of Rashbi: *Rabban* (252) *Shimon* (466) *Ben* (52) *Yochai* (35) = 805. In this way, Rashbi himself was the human rainbow of his generation, a manifest expression of Hashem's covenant with the world.

The spreading of the inner teachings of the Torah is what will awaken us to the reality of Moshiach. The rainbow itself is a physical symbol or harbinger of Moshiach. In the Zohar we read, "The rainbow that appears in the sky has a profound mystical significance, and when Israel will go forth from exile that rainbow is destined to be decked out in all the finery of its colors, like a bride who adorns herself for her husband… This is what my father said to me when he was on the point of departing this world: 'Do not expect the coming of the Moshiach until the rainbow appears decked out in resplendent colors which will illuminate the world. Only then expect Moshiach'" (*Zohar* 1, 72b).

Thus far we have associated the bow and arrow as a metaphor for the rainbow. But what does the bow and arrow represent in its own right, and what is its connection with Lag b'Omer?

Clearly, the bow and arrow is used as a weapon in battle, anyone can see that. Yet, what is most important and emphasized on Lag b'Omer is the *Penimyus* / inner, hidden dimension of Torah and life in general, and so, we need to understand the deeper connection between bows and arrows with Lag b'Omer.

Simply put, the advantage of the bow and arrow over the spear or sword is that it can reach its destination without personal encounter. Essentially, the distance an arrow travels is dependent on how far it was pulled back towards the archer. The closer you draw the arrow to yourself the further it flies. Essentially, the bow and arrow is an expression of a basic principle, "The higher the source, the lower it can travel." Concepts of spatial proximity such as 'near' and 'far,' 'higher' and 'lower,' are thus spiritually connected. This concept is intrinsically related to *Penimiyus haTorah* / inner dimension of Torah, the hidden light which illuminates our darkness.

On Lag b'Omer when we celebrate the Penimius haTorah, we play and shoot a bow and arrow, representing this dynamic; the further back the arrow is pulled, the further it flies in the opposite direction. The deeper you dig inward, the higher you climb, and the higher you reach, the more you can bring what you find into practical reality.

Lag b'Omer, as we explained earlier, is the peak of the Omer period, the point of super-majority. As this period is a time of separation and yearning to get closer to the 'wedding day' of Shavuos, the peak day is the point of greatest yearning. When lovers are together, it is called 'overt unity.' However, when they are yearning for each other while separated by a great distance, it is called 'hidden unity.' The further they are pulled apart, as with a bow and arrow, the stronger and more unstoppable is their inner drive to be together. This is, in a sense, an even deeper union, as it is not dependent on external conditions of physical proximity.

The act of shooting a bow and arrow on Lag b'Omer is an auspicious conduit for the blessing of having children (*Sefer haMidos*, Banim, 63). This is also alluded to in the verse:

"And the sons of Ulam were mighty men of valor, shooters of the *Keshes* קשת (archers); they had many sons, and sons' sons" (*Divrei haYamim* 1, 8:40).

It is known that Lag b'Omer is an auspicious time to pray for children, as Rashbi is connected to giving blessings for children[*] Many Chassidim would ask their Rebbes for blessings for children on Lag b'Omer. Perhaps this is connected with the general theme of Lag b'Omer, the deeper the separation, the deeper the longing you experience, the more unified you are with the goal. If a strong desire for children is the pulling back of the arrow, the release of the arrow is success in becoming pregnant. Similarly, a birth is preceded by contractions; the pulling back of the bow and the release of the arrow is the "birth of a child."

All prayers in general are related to this dynamic: the tension of feeling that we are missing something or are separated from something (pulling back the bow), followed by a sense of reunification or wholeness (releasing the arrow). Unkolus, the first and primary translator of Torah renders the words, "With my sword and my bow" (*Bereishis*, 48:22) as "with prayer and supplication."

Certain *Mekubalim* / Kabbalists write that by placing both hands upon one's heart in prayer we are forming a bow *(Pirush HaChayit, Ma'areches Elokus,* 10. See also: *Nefutzos Yehudah,* Derush 24). The hands laying one over the other creates an image of a bow underneath.

---

[*]*Medrash, Shir HaShirim*, 1:30. What is more, Rava said, "May every bearing mother bear a child like Rabbi Shimon." Rashi explains, when having a child we should pray, "may it be His will that this child grow up to be like Rabbi Shimon". *Makos,* 17b.

The hands are the bow and the arrow is the tongue. What pulls the bow back and thus releases the arrow forward with force is our *Kavanah* / inner intention. When we are praying we are sending arrows Above to pierce the Heavens, and draw down the flow of *Shefa* / abundance into our lives.

Indeed, the deeper we pull our prayers back into ourselves, and the more we can bear the spiritual tension and lack, the further our prayers can then reach, so to speak. The word *Keshes* can be seen as an acronym for *Shomeia* / the one who hears, *Kol* / the sound of *Tefiloseinu* / our prayers.

Lines and Circles

In life, our boundaries and limitations can be seen as lines, and the breaking out of these lines can be seen as circles. An arrow is a line, and the bow, when drawn back, forms a half circle. When we pull back the arrow on the bow, both a circular curve and a line are simultaneously present.

In a circle there is no beginning or end, there are no defined points. A line on the other hand, has a beginning and an end, and defined coordinates in between. In this way a line represents a state of being finite, defined, and reified, and a circle represents a state of being infinite and undefined.

A line represents *Din* and separation. The hair of one's head is also *Din* and separation, as no two hairs emerge from the same root, "I have created many hairs in a man's head and for every hair I have created a separate follicle" (*Niddah*, 52b). Every strand of hair is a distinct conduit of energy. A linear strand of hair is also shaped like the letter Vav (*Sha'ar haMitzvos*, Parshas Kedoshim), the letter that connects one point to another. However, a line of separation and limitation can also be a line of connection.

In a time of *Din* and linear reality such as the Omer, we refrain from cutting our hair. On Lag b'Omer, however, we are allowed to take haircuts, thus halting and limiting the encroachment of Din and a purely linear paradigm. Additionally, we take a line — a straight archer's bow— and make it into a circular curve. Then we pull back and let the line of the arrow fly toward its target; there is tremendous release and great joy on Lag b'Omer.

Prose and Poetry

A line also represents the prose, the defined storyline, of our life. A circle, on the other hand, represents the poetry, the non-linear aspect of our life. Law and order are linear, music and poetry are circular. The Torah is both; it has the linear aspect of law, and yet the Torah also refers to itself as a *Shira* / song (*Devarim*, 31:19). While this is true of the Torah in general, more specifically the *Niglah* / Revealed or Written Torah is seen as linear, being the laws of life that we accept from Above. The *Nistar* / Hidden and Oral Torah, those dimensions which are revealed through human participation, is circular in nature. Lag b'Omer, the revelation of the inner aspects of Torah, is therefore primarily a 'circle' day.

Customs such as the bow and arrow arise from the unconscious collective prophetic soul of *K'nesses Yisrael* / the gathering or totality of the People of Israel. This is true with regards to the Rabbinic *Yomim Tovim* / holidays in general. Lag b'Omer is not an official *Yom Tov*, and it is not found in the Torah or even clearly in the Gemara, rather it is a more 'modern' arising of the same deep collective wisdom which composes the Rabbinic holidays.

The two fully Rabbinic holidays in the calendar are Purim and Chanukah. Additionally, there is also a universally practiced celebration attached to the final day of Sukkos called *Simchas Torah*. This is another more 'modern' innovation, first found in the times of the Geonim. On all these days, there is a theme of rounding off, of creating a 'circle' out of something that is linear or square.

On Chanukah this occurs with the custom of spinning a Dreidel; the four linear sides of the Dreidel blur into a circle as it spins. On Purim, a very similar phenomenon occurs when we spin a *Gragger* / noise maker. On Simchas Torah, we dance with the Torah in circles around the square *Bimah* / reading table, which is an image of the Altar in the Holy Temple.

On Lag b'Omer we place the arrow of our longing into the bow of our being, and pull the string of our separation to its breaking point. The deeper we pull back the bow into ourselves, the higher our arrow will fly into the heart of the Beloved.

☾

PARADES

While in previous centuries it was common for people to go out into the fields or parks on Lag b'Omer to play with bows and arrows, today it has also become common to celebrate Lag b'Omer with parades and other public displays. Lag b'Omer is in part a celebration of the continuation of the Torah's transmission after the devastating death of the 24,000 students of Rabbi Akiva and the crushing defeat of the Bar Kochva revolt. The fact that neither Rabbi Akiva nor the People of Israel gave up after such losses is truly a cause for celebration. Although Rabbi Akiva's hope of global Redemption in his days was crushed with the betrayal of Bar Kochva and the death of his students, the emergence of Rashbi and the other four students of Rabbi Akiva embodies the flourishing of Torah, the *Mesora* / transmission of Torah, a further miracle which fill us with a renewed hope for the future.

As Rashbi emerged from his cave and began to bring the hidden *Penimius haTorah* into the open, this inspired others to go outside and celebrate publicly on Lag b'Omer. Perhaps this is part of the reason that soon after the devastating Holocaust in Europe, the Lubavitcher Rebbe of Blessed memory, encouraged Jews around the world to make parades with children on Lag b'Omer — openly and fearlessly celebrating Jewish pride, unity, continuity, and an unbreakable hope for Redemption. The Rebbe's request was clearly a call to openly reveal even more of the Torah's hidden light.

UPSHERIN

Upsherin is a ceremony celebrating a three-year-old boy's first haircut. The idea of Upsherin has almost become synonymous with Lag b'Omer. This is because during the period of the Omer cutting one's hair, as explored earlier is forbidden, except for on the day of Lag B'Omer. So any boy who turns three during this period should have his Upsherin on that day, and that is why there are many such celebrations on the day of Lag b'Omer.

Upsherin and Lag b'Omer have an affinity based on the fact that one of the earliest sources of this custom of Upsherin is found in the writings of the Arizal, who himself took his young son on Lag b'Omer to Meron, the gravesite of Rashbi, and gave him a haircut "according to the well-known tradition" (*Sha'ar Hakavanos*, Pesach, Derush 12. Note, *Teshuvas Radbaz* 2, Siman 608).

On a deeper level, the act of cutting hair and the energy of Lag b'Omer are intricately connected. The 49 days between Pesach and Shavuos represent 49 steps of personal development, preceded by the experience of freedom on Pesach, and followed by the assumption of the responsibility to keep the Torah on Shavuos. As we have explored, there are seven primary emotional *Sefiros* / personal attributes. Each of these attributes on its own without the counterbalance of the others creates a condition of *Tohu* / chaos or confusion. To establish *Tikkun* / correction and balance, we need to blend our attributes so that each one of the seven contains all of the others, creating a sum total of 49 combinations. Each day of the Omer, we work on creating the state of balance represented by that day's combination.

Lag b'Omer, the 33rd day, corresponds to the Sefirah-combination of *Hod shebeHod* / glory of glory. If we were to count backwards from 49, the Sefirah-combination of Lag b'Omer would be *Tiferes shebeTiferes* / beauty of beauty. Both of these Sefirah-combinations express a quality of perfect *Tikkun* and balance. As such, it is a most auspicious time to cut a young boy's hair, as the cutting of the hair (and the entering into the fourth year of life) represents the beginning of a balanced, orderly life.

The Omer offering was comprised of *Se'or* / barley, which was considered in the ancient Near East to be more of an animal feed than a food for humans (*Sotah* 14a). The offering of an animal food on the Altar represents Din, as it is for the unconscious actions of our animal soul that we most often bring sacrifices to the Temple. The word *Se'or*, has the same root letters as the word *Shiur* / measurement, alluding to Din, judgment, and boundaries. Both of these words share root letters with the word *Se'ir* / hair. We don't cut our *Se'ir* during the time we are offering *Se'or*, as we are still in an 'animal' reality. We can only cut our hair and thereby create proper Tikkun, when we are ready to become 'human' and offer the *Shtei haLechem* / Two Breads offering of Shavuos, which is made of wheat, an archetypal human food.

Long, wild male hair is an image and energy of *Tohu*, related to Eisav, "the hairy one." When this hair is cut, the boy's physical image is 'contained' or shaped, almost like a vessel. The spiritual energy of Tohu is thus focused and balanced. As a result of the hair-cutting, many boys immediately see themselves as more mature, balanced or noble, and their behavior follows suit.

ZOHAR STUDY AND SONGS IN HONOR OF RASHBI

Lag b'Omer is an opportune time to study the Zohar, especially sections of the Zohar that speak of the praise of Rashbi (*Avodas HaKodesh*, Morah b'Etzbah, 223). Many also have a custom to sing songs in honor of Rashbi. Learning mystical texts and singing holy songs are both ways that we can use our mouths in a holy manner, in a manner similar to Rashbi.* One of the more famous compositions sung on Lag b'Omer is called *Bar Yochai*, which was composed by Rav Shimon Ben Labia some 450 years ago. Another song that is sung throughout the world today is called *VaAmartem Ko leChai* composed by the venerable Sefardic sage, the Ben Ish Chai (1832- 1909) in honor of Rashbi.

---

* The Rashbi, was very careful with how and when he spoke. Regarding Shabbos, see *Pesikta Rabsi*, Parsha 23:3. *Tosefos*, Shabbos, 113b. *Medrash Rabbah*, Vayikra, 34:16. Regarding causing another person pain through words, see, *Baba Metziyah*, 58b. Regarding being careful that others do not become lax with vows, see *Nedarim*, 66b. Rashbi once said, that if he was at the giving of the Torah, he would have prayed (initially, although he changed his mind) that Hashem would give man two mouths, one to speak Torah, and the other to speak mundane words. Yerushalmi, *Berachos*, 1:2.

A third popular song is composed of a collage of Rabbi Akiva's own words in the Mishnah: *Amar Rabbi Akiva*. This song is meant to arouse the *Zechus* / merit of Rabbi Akiva, who was the Rebbe of Rashbi and the Tzadik who is fundamentally related to the whole concept of Sefiras haOmer. Since the words of this Mishnah speak of purification, the song is a celebration of our ongoing purification process throughout the Omer period, and the preparation of our vessels for the receiving of Torah on Shavuos.

Bar Yochai

בַּר-יוֹחַאי, נִמְשַׁחְתָּ - אַשְׁרֶיךָ
שֶׁמֶן שָׂשׂוֹן מֵחֲבֵרֶיךָ

[Refrain between each verse]
Bar Yochai! You were anointed — fortunate are you — with oil of gladness, for the sake of your companions.

בַּר-יוֹחַאי, שֶׁמֶן מִשְׁחַת קֹדֶשׁ
נִמְשַׁחְתָּ מִמִּדַּת הַקֹּדֶשׁ
נָשָׂאתָ צִיץ נֵזֶר הַקֹּדֶשׁ
חָבוּשׁ עַל רֹאשְׁךָ פְּאֵרֶךָ

[Verse 1: Malchus]
Bar Yochai! With oil of sacred anointment
You drew from the holy vessel.
You wore the golden head-plate, the diadem of holiness;
Bound upon your head, your beauty.

בַּר-יוֹחַאי, מוֹשַׁב טוֹב יָשַׁבְתָּ
יוֹם נַסְתָּ, יוֹם אֲשֶׁר בָּרַחְתָּ
בִּמְעָרַת צוּרִים שֶׁעָמַדְתָּ
קָנִיתָ הוֹדְךָ וַהֲדָרֶךָ

[Verse 2: Yesod]
Bar Yochai! To a good dwelling did you retreat
On the day you ran, the day you fled.
In a cave among the cliffs you remained;
There you acquired your brilliance and your splendor.

בַּר-יוֹחַאי, עֲצֵי שִׁטִּים עוֹמְדִים
לִמּוּדֵי ד' הֵם לוֹמְדִים
אוֹר מֻפְלָא, אוֹר הַיְקוֹד הֵם יוֹקְדִים
הֲלֹא הֵמָּה יוֹרוּךָ מוֹרֶךָ

[Verse 3: Netzach and Hod]
Bar Yochai! Like standing acacia beams in the Tabernacle,
Hashem's disciples engage in study.
With wondrous light, with fiery light, they burn —
Behold, your teachers, who shall instruct you!

בַּר-יוֹחַאי, וְלִשְׂדֵה תַּפּוּחִים
עָלִיתָ לִלְקֹט בּוֹ מֶרְקָחִים
סוֹד תּוֹרָה בְּצִיצִים וּפְרָחִים
נַעֲשֶׂה אָדָם נֶאֱמַר בַּעֲבוּרֶךָ

[Verse 4: Tiferes]
Bar Yochai! To the Field of Apples you ascended
To gather precious things from afar,
Mysteries of Torah like blossoms and flowers.
"Let Us make man" was said because of you!

Customs and Practices of Lag B'Omer | 163

בַּר-יוֹחַאי, נֶאֱזַרְתָּ בִּגְבוּרָה
וּבְמִלְחֶמֶת אֵשׁ דָּת הַשַּׁעְרָה
וְחֶרֶב הוֹצֵאתָ מִתַּעְרָהּ
שָׁלַפְתָּ נֶגֶד צוֹרְרֶיךָ

[Verse 5: Gevurah]
Bar Yochai! You were girded with strength,
And in the battle of the "Fiery Law," at the city's gate,
Your sword you drew from its scabbard,
Wielding it against (your People's self-appointed) enemies.

בַּר-יוֹחַאי, לִמְקוֹם אַבְנֵי שַׁיִשׁ
הִגַּעְתָּ וּפְנֵי אַרְיֵה לַיִשׁ
גַּם גֻּלַּת כּוֹתֶרֶת עַל עַיִשׁ
תָּשׁוּר וּמִי יְשׁוּרֶךָ

[Verse 6: Chesed]
Bar Yochai! The visionary Place of Marble Stones
You reached, and came before the Supernal Lion.
Even the orb of the crown set upon the star Arcturus
You beheld — but none can behold you!

בַּר-יוֹחַאי, בְּקֹדֶשׁ הַקֳּדָשִׁים
קַו יָרֹק מְחַדֵּשׁ חֳדָשִׁים
שֶׁבַע שַׁבָּתוֹת סוֹד חֲמִשִּׁים
קָשַׁרְתָּ קִשְׁרֵי שִׁי"ן קְשָׁרֶיךָ

[Verse 7: Binah]
Bar Yochai! In the Holy of Holies —
The "green line" that creates new manifestations —
Seven Sabbaths, the secret of 50,
You fastened the bonds of the letter Shin as your bonds!

בַּר-יוֹחַאי, יוּ"ד חָכְמָה קְדוּמָה
הִשְׁקַפְתָּ לִכְבוּדָהּ פְּנִימָה
לְ"ב נְתִיבוֹת רֵאשִׁית תְּרוּמָה
אֵתְּ כְּרוּב מִמְשַׁח זִיו דּוֹרֶךָ

[Verse 8: Chochmah]
Bar Yochai! The Yud of primordial wisdom
You gazed into its innermost glory;
The 32 Paths, the exalted point of origin.
You are a cherub anointed, the radiance of your generation!

בַּר-יוֹחַאי, אוֹר מֻפְלָא רָם מַעְלָה
יָרֵאתָ מִלְּהַבִּיט כִּי רַב לָהּ
תַּעֲלוּמָה וְאַיִן קֹרָא לָהּ
נַמְתָּ: עַיִן לֹא תְשׁוּרֶךָ

[Verse 9: Keser]
Bar Yochai! The wondrous light that shines above
You feared to glimpse, for it is vast.
Divine mystery, "Ayin (No-thingness)" she is called.
Indeed, you declared, "No eye shall see You."

בַּר-יוֹחַאי, אַשְׁרֵי יוֹלַדְתֶּךָ
אַשְׁרֵי הָעָם לוֹמְדֶיךָ
וְאַשְׁרֵי הָעוֹמְדִים עַל סוֹדֶךָ
לוֹבְשֵׁי חֹשֶׁן תֻּמֶּיךָ וְאוּרֶיךָ

[Verse 10]
Bar Yochai! Fortunate is she who bore you,
Fortunate is the people that learns from you,
Fortunate are those who can fathom your mystery,
Garbed in the Priestly Breastplate, Your sacred oracle!

Amar Rabbi Akiva, Ashreichem Yisrael
(Yuma 84b, Mishnah)

אָמַר רַבִּי עֲקִיבָא: אַשְׁרֵיכֶם יִשְׂרָאֵל!	Rabbi Akiva said: Happy are you, People of Israel!
לִפְנֵי מִי אַתֶּם מִיטַּהֲרִין? מִי מְטַהֵר אֶתְכֶם?	Before Whom do you cleanse yourself? And who cleanses you?
אֲבִיכֶם שֶׁבַּשָּׁמַיִם!	Your Father in Heaven!
שֶׁנֶּאֱמַר: וְזָרַקְתִּי עֲלֵיכֶם מַיִם טְהוֹרִים וּטְהַרְתֶּם	As it says (Yechezkel, 36:25), "And I will sprinkle you with pure waters and you will be purified,"
וְאוֹמֵר: "מִקְוֵה יִשְׂרָאֵל ה'."	And it also says (Yirmiyahu, 17:13), "The *mikveh* of Yisrael is Hashem."
מַה מִּקְוֶה מְטַהֵר אֶת הַטְּמֵאִים, אַף הַקָּדוֹשׁ בָּרוּךְ הוּא מְטַהֵר אֶת יִשְׂרָאֵל	Just as a *mikveh* cleanses the contaminated, so does The Holy One Blessed Be He cleanse Yisrael.

Chapter Three

ESSAYS ON THE OMER & LAG B'OMER

1) Creating Balance through Counting the Omer

2) *Hod shebeHod / Splendor of Splendor*

3) Longing to See the Face of *Elokim*

4) *Unifying Separation*

CREATING BALANCE THROUGH COUNTING THE OMER

While the Torah itself does not offer a rationale for counting the days between Pesach and Shavuos, the Medrash does. The Medrash relates that when we left Egypt we knew that eventually we were going to receive the Torah and so we counted the days until that event in great anticipation (*RaN*, Pesachim, Chapter 10). We too, having achieved liberation from our own personal 'Egypt' and limitations on the holiday of Pesach, count the days leading up to once again receiving the Torah on Shavuos. The 'freedom from' Egypt on Pesach is only meaningful in the context of the Torah revelation. For it is the Torah that gives us the tools and 'freedom to' reach our ultimate destination of justice, truth, and universal peace — the intention and purpose of the liberation from Egypt.

The Torah mentions the Exodus from Egypt 50 times. According to the Zohar (2, 85b), these 50 mentions correspond to the 50 days of Sefirah, i.e., the 49 that we count, plus one for the day of Shavuos. The 49 intermediate days are not just 'spacerholders,' bridging Passover and Shavuos. The daily count-down in anticipation of Shavuos involves 49 integral steps on the path of liberating oneself from within, in order to deeply receive the Torah. Each day is an important end in itself. One cannot authentically reach the '50th Gate' of revelation without first opening the previous 49 gates within oneself.

Each of the 49 days is a level of personal development, traversing seven *Sefiros* / attributes or areas of self-rectification: *Chesed* / giving, *Gevurah* / restraint, *Tiferes* / harmony, *Netzach* / ambition, *Hod* / devotion, *Yesod* / connectivity, and *Malchus* / receptivity.

To open and free ourselves to receive Revelation, each of our seven attributes needs to be balanced out by each one of the other attributes. Let us take, for example, the first attribute, *Chesed* / giving and kindness. Imagine generosity without any counterbalance of *Gevurah* / restraint. For example; You are walking down the street and you notice a small child playing with a sharp knife. If your *Chesed* is not balanced with *Gevurah*, you might 'generously' allow the child to play with the knife. But of course this is not real generosity, it is foolishness. It is even selfish — perhaps you do not want to be the 'bad guy' who takes away a toy and makes someone else's child cry. Real kindness would mean showing Gevurah; taking the knife away and notifying his parent or giving the child an appropriate toy.

To live in freedom and productivity we need to cultivate a state of harmony and synergy between the often vying attributes within. The word "liberated" comes from the Greek word *Libra* / balance. To be liberated is to be properly balanced. In order to cultivate *Tikkun* and balance within a chaotic world we need to establish a conscious, organized interplay, and combination of our inner forces.

A balanced synthesis of our *Sefiros* is achieved via *Hamshachas Mochin b'Midos* / drawing down higher intelligence into our emotional qualities and responses. If we habitually allow our emotional reactions to take hold over us, causing us to lash out or shut down unconsciously, we are likely to harm others as well as ourselves. We therefore need to work on bringing a measure of *Mochin* / intelligence and *Yishuv haDa'as* / settling of consciousness into different aspects of our internal system. Each day of the Omer we work in this way on another aspect of our emotional reality, aligning our *Midos* to operate as an intimate, intelligent, unified team. Chesed is channeled by Gevurah and Gevurah is humanized by Chesed. By counting and meditating on the spiritual quality of each day all of the *Sefiros* synergistically combine and refine one another until they all together form a single chariot of blessing.

As discussed, the Omer period is characterized as a period of mourning. Clearly in a time of introspection, self-evaluation, and change there ought to be a level of seriousness and sincerity — but why sadness or mourning? And why, in the middle of such mourning, is there suddenly a day of great joy and celebration?

As we have learned, the Gemara recounts that some 1,800 years ago between Passover and Shavuos, 24,000 of Rabbi Akiva's students died from a mysterious plague. It says they died because they "did not act respectfully towards each other." And this is the reason for the grief.

The troubling oddity of this story is that these were the dedicated students of Rabbi Akiva, he who famously proclaimed, "Loving your fellow as yourself is the great principle of the Torah." If they ignored or even despised Rabbi Akiva's most essential teaching and principle, how can they even be referred to as his "students?"

The answer is, these students suffered from exactly what we mentioned above. They did indeed 'love' each other, and they had cultivated a high level of *Chesed*. The trouble was that they wanted to give without the balance of *Gevurah*; without sensitively withholding, even when the receiver was not open to receive.

Their disrespect was not because they lacked love for each other, rather the opposite. They loved one another with such intense emotion, they wished to share all their dreams, ideas, and ambitions with each other, at any cost. Most of us feel motivated to share with others our most cherished values, insights, and gifts in life. However, as each student attempted to impart to the others what he deemed was most valuable, he did not take notice that others had their own dreams, beliefs, and values. He therefore did not notice when his sharing had become a burden to the other rather than an appreciated gift, which it was blindly intended to be. Thus they expressed Chesed without Gevurah; kindness without boundaries, giving without respect.

Parents naturally try to give all they have, and even what they themselves didn't have, to their children. The risk is, in the process they might impose themselves and overwhelm / stifle the child's own individuality. Proper giving includes respecting the receiver, and that sometimes demands practicing restraint and non-interference.

We must learn from the students of Rabbi Akiva to eliminate arrogance and insensitive imposition from our giving. To effectively balance and integrate our Chesed and Gevurah, as well as all the other emotional states; we need to count, measure, and inspect each combination of Midos individually. It also helps to bring to mind what could occur if there were an imbalance in a given Midah during a certain situation. What would be the effect if my *Chesed* were lacking *Yesod* / connectivity, or *Malchus* / receptivity? We can also reflect on and 'mourn' our past imbalanced thoughts, words, and deeds. Mourning is not depression or self-inflicted anger, rather, it is an 'acceptance of failure' which energizes, balances, and liberates us.

Sefirah / counting the 49 combinations, brings about a *Tikkun* and rebalancing of every possible psycho-emotional attribute. The *Sefiros* then become *Sapir* / shining, like a *sapphire*; our emotional centers gradually become settled, self-aware, and shining with higher intelligence. Then, every thought, word, and deed can be a vessel or conduit of blessing, and we are ready, once again, to receive the Torah — the Ultimate Blessing. Only when this balance and alignment has been completely achieved, can Torah truly flow through us to others, in a way they can receive.

Lag b'Omer: The Day of Balance

Lag b'Omer stands out as a refuge of joy amid a time of semi-mourning and sadness.

Beyond being a prime student of the illustrious Rabbi Akiva, Rashbi once told his own disciples, "My sons, learn my ways, for my ways are the finest of the finest of Rabbi Akiva's." He was a great person in his own right. His specialness is also illustrated by the fact that while the other students died, he survived, and only passed away once he had reached a ripe old age. It was Rashbi himself who requested of his people to dedicate the day of his passing as, "the day of my joy."

There are no coincidences; everything is Divinely orchestrated and organized. What we need to explore is the connection between his celebratory death, the mournful death of the students, and how both of these phenomena relate to the counting of the Omer.

As we understood above, an overarching theme of the Omer is the balancing and integration of our emotional states. The most extreme emotions are aroused in a time of tragedy on one hand, and in a time of comedy on the other. In both cases, we are thrown something unexpected. Whether it is unexpectedly good or not, our instinctual responses are awakened and we react without awareness or intentionality. We thus lose our inner balance, alignment, and proactive *Kochos* / abilities.

The death of a loved one (G-d forbid) stirs within us deep emotions of sadness. In fact, the *Rambam* / Maimonides says that a person who does not show sadness in the face of death is an *Achzar*

/ a cruel cold-hearted person (*Hilchos Avel*, 13:12). The root of the word *Achzar* is *Zar* / foreigner, stranger. An *Achzar* is someone who is distant from others specifically, and natural life in general. Not only are we meant to mourn, we are encouraged to weep and bewail a death. The first three days of *Shiva* are called 'the days of weeping.' There is a time for sadness — not despondency or thinking that one's life is over — but real, vulnerable sadness.

And yet, in the midst of the Omer, a national time of semi-mourning, Lag b'Omer appears, a day of fiery elation. The effect of this unusually swift change of mood is meant to counter-balance our previous 32 days of mourning; to get us out of our 'funk.' Mourning is not meant to be our psychological status quo or automatic default feeling about our lives or the world. Too much focus on the negative could very easily lead to a kind of callousness or 'cold-heartedness.' We are thus guided, by means of the soul of Rashbi, to diligently work on being present, sensitive, and balanced within ourselves, so that our responses and reactions to what life throws at us will be conscious, creative, and compassionate.

It is precisely the mystic par excellence, the illustrious Rashbi, the one who looks beyond immediate appearances, who can guide us in this way. He shows us that even death can be a time of rejoicing. When something looks like an end, he reveals the possibility of 'continuation' or even the beginning of a bright future. If something seems bad in the moment, it may turn out to be good later. What seems to be an exile can also be a hidden homecoming. The very fact that we celebrate on the day Rashbi died suggests that we are starting to see a bit deeper, beneath the surface, into the *Penimius* of life. We are being shown a glimpse of the truly celebratory nature of life that is 'inter-included' with sadness and loss.

Lag b'Omer is on *Chai Iyyar* / (the 18th day or) aliveness of Iyyar. This single day infuses the Omer, an extended period of collective mourning, with a necessary dose of life and hope. Aliveness is by nature sensitive, flexible, optimistic, and balanced. As these qualities begin to vivify the month of Iyyar, they also radiate into all the days of our lives.

HOD SHEBEHOD / SPLENDOR OF SPLENDOR

When the ten Sefiros are mapped onto the human body, the Sefirah of *Hod* / splendor corresponds to the left leg or thigh. Lag b'Omer is the Hod *within* Hod, the *inner* quality of the left leg. To understand this dynamic, let us first look at this day's theoretical 'mirror reflection' within the Omer count. Theoretically, if the days of Sefirah would be counted from the bottom up — from Malchus to Chesed — the 33rd day of the Sefirah would be *Tiferes shebeTiferes* / beauty of beauty. There is a deep correspondence between the Sefiros of Tiferes and Hod. Hod is sometimes called *Chein* / grace or charm. It is a humble but radiant spiritual beauty deep inside, behind a person's surface appearance.

Ya'akov is the definitive embodiment of Tiferes, thus, regarding Ya'akov our Sages mention beauty, "The beauty of Ya'akov was reminiscent of the beauty of Adam" (*Baba Metziyah*, 84a). When Ya'akov wrestled with the Angel of Esav he was injured in the place of the *Yerech* / thigh, "When he saw that he prevailed not against him, he touched the hollow of his thigh, and the hollow of Ya'akov's thigh went out of joint" (*Bereishis*, 32:26). Thus the Angel of Esav damages his attribute of Hod.[*] Although Ya'akov still had his outer 'beauty' intact, his *Chein* / inner beauty had been 'dislocated.' The angel was not so concerned that Ya'akov had the outer beauty of Tiferes, many people have that. He felt that the real way to wound or impair Ya'akov would be to damage him on the level of Hod, so that he would not be aware of his own inner beauty, his *Chein*.

Beauty shines from the inside out. If a person feels inwardly beautiful, they project themselves that way. Inner beauty is also humble; it is not so prone to entanglement with ego as outward beauty can be. Someone with Hod or Chein is able to humbly receive constructive criticism. When someone wants to help you or improve you, it takes Chein to accept their words. The Chein of Hod is therefore the antidote to the distorted behaviors of the 24,000 students whose inner humility was 'dislocated' in their lack of respect.

---

[*] *Pardes Rimonim* 17:1. *Siddur Kol Ya'akov*, Chanukah. Alter Rebbe, *Siddur Im Dach*, Derush Lag b'Omer. The damage was in Netzach, but permeated also the level of Hod. Arizal, *Sha'ar Ma'amorei Rashbi*, Bereishis, 13a. See also, *Likutei Torah*, Arizal, Vayishlach. There is debate in the Gemara regarding whether only the right thigh or both thighs were injured. *Chulin*, 91a. See, D*erech Mitzvosecho*, Gid Hanoshe.

Lag b'Omer, the energy of *Hod shebeHod*, helps us restore the splendor of our inner beauty. As soon as we 'count' and realize the rectification of this inner attribute, great flames of joy can burst forth from within us. The bonfires we light on Lag b'Omer are thus the external manifestations of this inner light being rekindled and revealed. The light of this fire allows us to see through the darkness of night to a glorious aliveness that can never die.

LONGING TO SEE THE FACE OF ELOKIM

During the 49 days of the Omer we yearn and aspire to reach Matan Torah. Yearning is an experience of Din, and thus the 49 days are an expression of the Name *Elokim*, as will be explained. Lag b'Omer is the moment when we have made it through two thirds of the 49 days of the Omer. Then begin the last 17 days, the number 17 being the numerical value of the word *Tov* / good. Thus from the day of Lag b'Omer onwards there is a shift from mourning into a refined perception of goodness within the Din, which serves to 'sweeten' our judgments. Once we have put in the effort to work hard on ourselves and achieve the necessary *Tikkunim* up until the fifth day of the fifth week (Lag b'Omer), Hashem will then step in and complete the *Tikkun* for us (*Beis Ya'akov* (Ishbitz) Parshas Bechukosai).

During the first 32 days of the Omer we are very much in the state of consciousness represented by the verse *Tzama Nafshi l'Elohim, l'E-l Chai, Masai Avo v'Eira'eh P'nei Elo-him* / My soul thirsts (yearns) for Elokim, for the Living G-d; when will I come and see the Face of Elokim (*Tehilim* 63:2).* Says the Maggid of Koznitz (*Avodas Yisrael*), Lag b'Omer is the time of *Hamtakas Din* / sweetening of judgment, because it is the revealing of the *P'nei Elokim* / the inner face of G-d's *Din*.

Elokim is the Divine Name associated with *Din* / judgment. *P'nei Elokim* / the Face of Elokim is thus the inner essence of judgment. The root word of *P'nei* can also mean 'inside' (as in *Penimiyus*) and 'prior to' (as in *Lif'nei*).

Let us look deeper into our verse. "My soul longs…*l'Kel Chai* / to the living G-d." The phrase *Kel Chai* is numerically 31 + 18 = 49. During these 49 days between Pesach and Shavuos we yearn for the revelation of the Living G-d, which is Matan Torah (See Ran in the name of the Medrash, end of Pesachim). We yearn to be fully alive, to get out of our *Tumah* / our deadening impurity or stagnant state of separation; we yearn for living unity. On the day of Lag b'Omer we finally reach the point where we can glimpse the *P'nei Elokim* / Inner Face of Elokim. The intense longing of the prior 32 days actually reveals the *Lev* (32) / the inner heart of connectivity and unity within the Din of the Omer. The Inner Face of Elokim is the goodness hidden behind the mask of apparent harsh judgment.

---

* During Sefiras haOmer we are also connected to the message of Tehilim 67. In Psalm 67 there are 49 words (besides the opening verse "For the Conductor…"), that is why we recite this chapter following the counting of the Omer. In fact, the 33rd word of the chapter is the name *Elokim*.

Lag b'Omer is 'the Face of Elokim' — the reality that exists inside and prior to the Din of Elokim. According to the practice of letter permutation and substitution, the 'inner' letters of the word *Elokim* (*Elo-him*) are the ones that immediately precede its letters. When we exchange the normal letters of the word with its preceding letters, the number 33 (Lag) is revealed.

To demonstrate: The first letter of *Elokim* is Aleph. Since this is the first letter of the Aleph Beis, there is no preceding letter, so we don't exchange it. The next letter in *Elokim* is Lamed. The letter preceding Lamed in the Aleph Beis is Chaf, so we exchange it and note its value of 20. The third letter is Hei, and the preceding letter is Dalet, with a value of 4. The next letter is Yud, with the preceding letter being Tes (9). The last letter is the 'Final Mem,' and the preceding letter in the full Aleph Beis is the regular Mem, so we do not exchange it. Only the three middle (or 'inner') letters — Lamed, Hei, and Yud — are exchanged, becoming Chaf, Dalet, and Tes, the sum of which is 33.

Essentially, the letters that precede each letter of the name Elokim reveal more *Rachamim* / compassion. This is because as they precede the manifest letters they are closer to their Source (*Sha'ar haKavanos*, Derush 2, Pesach), and thus convey less Din. Put another way, as the 'lower' letters of *Elokim*, these letters represent a weaker form of the energy of *Elokim*, which is Din.

With the exchanged inner letters, the new spelling is *ach-detam*, and in the deeper teachings of the Torah, this is referred to as the 'Divine Name *Achdetam*.' By contrast, the letters that follow each letter of *Elokim* reveal even more Din than *Elokim*: *Be-mu-*

chan. This is referred to as the 'Divine Name *b'Muchan*.'*

According to the Arizal (*Sefer haGilgulim*, Chapter 41), Lag b'Omer is connected with the Name *Achdetam*. Through this Name there is *Hamtakas Dinim* / sweetening of judgments. *Elokim* is the paradigm of separation and multiplicity, the sense that Hashem is hiding from us. However, the inner Face or essence of Elokim, represented by *Achdetam*, is a Divine kindness that is immeasurable — it is too intense to be revealed. However, on Lag b'Omer (*Lag* spells the word *Gal* / reveal) this inner essence is revealed in a way that we can access and internalize.

What is revealed on Lag/*Gal* b'Omer is that despite very real appearances, there is no actual hiding nor separation. All the constrictions and barriers in life are imaginary facades given to us for our ultimate benefit. For example, Hashem warns in the Torah, "I will surely hide from you..." (*Devarim*, 31:18). But when we become aware that it is Hashem's 'I' that is hiding — that even in hiddenness there is still "I, Hashem;" then we know Hashem is, has been, and always will be present all along.

The purpose of 'hiding' was paradoxically our realization that there is no place where Hashem is not present. Without the facade of hiding, we would not have been able to receive this revelation. We have to experience Elokim before we can experience the Inner Face of Elokim. The sweetening of Din is in the recognition that the sole purpose of separation is to bring out a deeper level of Unity. The experience of longing, exile, or death, is the medium through which this deeper unity is revealed.

---

* All of the above is in contrast to the same treatment given to the Name *Hashem* (YKVK); the preceding letters and the following letters of the Name Hashem, both reveal Din.

Lag b'Omer, A Day of Bitachon / Trust

In the midst of a prolonged period of mourning, introspection, and heaviness, Lag b'Omer gives us new strength and sweetens our Din. It shines light from within our darkness, so that we can shine our light out into the world in a healing and holy way. Eventually, we can fully appreciate and trust that the Light of Hashem is ever present even in the deepest darkness. To thrive in life with its many twists and turns we need this *Bitachon* / trust or confidence, this strength to never give up hope.

The Chasom Sofer writes that Lag b'Omer is the day the Mon starting falling. The Gemara teaches that each day the people had to go out and gather new Mon for that day. This situation required and stimulated *Bitachon* / Trust that Hashem would provide for them each day. "…Thus they were found to daily turn their attention to their Father in Heaven" (*Yumah*, 76a). In other words, the intention of the Mon, simply put, was to train the people to receive from Above — and the manner in which the Mon descended created longing, attentiveness, and *Bitachon* toward the One Above.

Rashbi did not give up Bitachon when he was secluded for 13 years in a cave. He believed he would survive, and he did. We could say that the miracles that occurred and fulfilled all his needs came as an effect of his trust: light, water, and food all manifested spontaneously in the cave. The *Charuv* / carob tree that grew for him by the mouth of the cave is comparable to the Mon in the desert. Rashbi also trusted that his seclusion was not an accident and that he was not a 'victim.' This enabled him to use the opportunity to study, meditate, and make a radical spiritual breakthrough. And he was able to do all this even while he was being sustained by carobs, which are (normally) "always harmful" (Rambam, *Hilchos De'os*, 4:11), but to him, with his Bitachon intact, they were were life saving and sustaining.

"Torah was only given to those who ate the Mon" (*Mechilta, Beshalach*). Mon is thus connected with Torah and with Rashbi, who reveals the deepest secrets of Torah on Lag b'Omer. We too need to have trust that Hashem will provide for all our needs that any sense of privation is ultimately for the purpose of our best spiritual interest. That every situation in life comes to us specifically as a tailor-made opportunity to 'receive the Torah' that we need to grow. We need to remind ourselves again and again that nothing is random, but is designed purposefully by the Infinite Source of compassion and wisdom. We have the choice to live in despair and anger or in the humble peace of Bitachon. Bitachon is what gives us an aura of *Chein* / inner grace and beauty. This is the inner quality of Lag b'Omer.

The name *Achdetam*, as we discussed earlier, is numerically related to the word *Bitachon*: Aleph/1 + Chaf /20 + Daled/4 + Tes/9 + Mem/40 equal 74 — the value of the words *Ad*, of *Bitchu Adei Ad* / until limitless Bitachon. The numerical value of *Achdetam* plus the *Kollel* / value of 1 for the word itself, is 75, the value of the word *Bitachon* itself (Beis/2 + Tes/9 + Ches/8 + Vav/6 + Nun/50 = 75).

Again, the value of *Achdetam* without the *Kollel* is 74, and this is the same value as the word *Eid* (עד) / witness. When Ya'akov and Lavan make a truce between themselves they erected a monument, saying that the *Gal* / pile of stones will be an *Eid* to their truce

(*Bereishis*, 31:48). As we mentioned above, the three letters that were exchanged to form the Name *Achdetam* add up to 33. This is also the value of the word *Gal*. The 33rd day of the Omer is a 'witness' to a truce or a 'sweetening' made between ourselves and the forces of harsh Din.

Bitchu b'Hashem Adei Ad may also be read as, "Trust Hashem until *Ad*." The word *Ad* (spelled the same as Eid) equals 74. Read in this way, the verse says, 'Trust in Hashem until you reach the *Ad* / the 74, which is *Achdatam*, the inner Face of Elokim, which brings a great sweetening of Din.'

Beyond the level of trust described above, we even need to have trust in trust itself. The verse, "Trust Hashem until *Ad* / 74," which is the value of the Name Achdatam, the archetypal Name of trust, means that even when we do not feel Bitachon, we should still trust in Hashem until we do. This ability to generate a degree of Bitachon even when we do not feel it strongly, will prepare our vessels to receive an influx of a higher level of Bitachon. But even when we are not feeling that level of trust, we can have trust in the process and patterns of Hashem's creation, and know that Bitachon will indeed return.

Rashbi and his son trusted Hashem in a 'limitless' way and were completely supported. When we left Egypt, we too had faith; we trusted Hashem and we went out of Egypt with no food or provisions. Later, the Prophet Yirmiyahu prophesied saying, "I remember the affection of your youth…when you followed Me into the wilderness…" (2:2). In other words, 'You trusted in Me.' Hod of Hod is the deepest level of humility and trust in Hashem. Lag b'Omer gives us the power to have limitless surrender to Hashem and to the wisdom of Hashem's plan for us even when it seems hidden behind a mask of Din.

Now we can perhaps understand something of the radical statement of the Zohar (2, 38) associating Rashbi himself with the P'nei Elokim (Hashem): "Whose is the face of the Master, the Divine? This is Rashbi." The face of the light that shines within darkness.

UNIFYING SEPARATION

When we count the days of the Sefirah we are placing our attention on units of time that are different and separate from one another. Generally speaking, past, present, and future are distinct, separate zones. Time appears to be a force of separation and fracture, causing loss, mourning, and Din.

On the other hand, the Torah asks us to count *Sheva Shabbasos Temimos* / seven whole weeks — we are thereby making seven separate weeks into one *Tamimus* / wholeness. The Mitzvah to count the Omer is a Mitzvah to count time itself. It is therefore perhaps not a Mitzvah that is 'time bound.' In fact it is not that time causes the Mitzvah, rather, the Mitzvah itself counts and thus creates time. Accordingly, we can now understand the seemingly paradoxical opinion of the Ramban (Ramban, *Kidushin*, 33b), who writes that the counting of the Omer is not a "time bound" Mitzvah, even though the Mitzvah is clearly to count from the second day of Pesach until Shavuos. By consciously counting and creating a new paradigm of time, we are unifying or healing the fractures of time — as in yesterday, today, and tomorrow — creating a singular wholeness of time out of separate units.

The *Halachah* (guidance in walking the path of Torah) states: The fact that we make a new *Berachah* / blessing on the Omer every day, indicates that each night is a new Mitzvah. Yet, if we miss one day, we cannot continue to count with a Berachah.* The process of counting the Omer is not all one Mitzvah, for if it were, why would we say a new blessing each night? But if this is true, why can't we continue counting with a blessing if we miss one day of counting? The reason for this ruling, is because [if we miss a day] we would be missing the *Temimus* / wholeness — you cannot count 1, 2, 3, and then 5; you need the 4. Therefore, we can see that we need to count each individual day on its own in order to then unify it with all the other days into a higher concept of holistic time.

Creating wholeness and unity out of separate parts is a perfect preparation and introduction to Matan Torah. When we, a

---

* The Behag writes that if you miss a single day counting do not continue counting, at all. Retorts *Tosefos*, (*Menachos*, 66a) "This is a great wonder, and it is not possible!" As quoted in the name of Rav Hai Gaon, "If one eats foul odored foods today should he do so again tomorrow?" The practical halacha provides a middle-ground of sorts, if you miss counting the Omer in the evening, you should count the following day, but without a blessing. Then, on subsequent nights, continue counting with a blessing as usual. The blessing is made only if every day has been counted. If you entirely missed counting a day, you should return to reciting the day's count, but without a blessing.

group of former slaves, had left Egypt and began counting down to Matan Torah, we were also learning how to be independent of the rhythms imposed upon us by our masters. In addition to counting the Omer, we were therefore also given the very first Mitzvah of declaring the New Moon as soon as we left Egypt, which ran on a solar calendar. We needed to recover our autonomy and re-learn how to manage and direct our own time. We needed to remember what it meant to have a goal, and to count down* to this goal with yearning and anticipation. Time became imbued with meaning again, which healed our inner fragmentation and made us whole. Finally, we were ready to receive the Torah, the revelation of meaningfulness, and wholeness in every aspect of life.

The purpose of Torah is to infuse creation with the recognition of Oneness. Iyyar's astrological sign of the bull alludes to the process of developing individuality. After Pesach, as newly redeemed slaves, we have to reclaim our authentic selves. We therefore count each day as an individual unit. However, the counting also creates a unification of disparate parts. Finally, we reach Sivan and the giving of the Torah, and arrive at Mt. Sinai, "as one individual with one heart." Our inner work on creating oneness below allows us to receive and integrate the empowering teaching of Oneness that descends from Above.

---

*Many Rishonim specify that it was a count-down, i.e. in anticipation of a goal. See *RaN*, Pesachim, at the end in the name of the Medrash. Additionally, we count up from one, two, until 49, and not in the reverse, from 49 to one, so as not to mention how long we have until Matan Torah. Ibid, *Sefer Hachinuch*, Mitzvah 306.

Lag b'Omer & Humility

Iyyar's theme of individuality describes our journey toward greater self-actualization. When we reach the fifth week of the Omer count, we turn to embodying the attribute of humility. On Lag b'Omer, the fifth day of the fifth week, we reach the embodiment of the deepest humility. This is the vital step in refining and aligning our sense of individuality.

Each of the seven weeks of Sefirah are related to one of the seven emotional Sefiros. The fifth week is Hod / humility. Lag b'Omer, the fifth day of the fifth week, is the Sefirah of *Hod shebeHod*. As a concept, the 'fifth' is generally related to giving thanks — another translation of the word *Hod*. According to one opinion in the Medrash, the angels were created on Thursday, the fifth day. The occupation of angels is to sing praise and thanks to the Creator. The Fifth day of creation is also the creation of the animals. Animals, like angels, have an innate 'humility,' doing only what they were created to do.

There are five *Kolos* / sounds that a person merits when bringing joy to a groom and bride. The fifth, is *Hodu* / thanks: 1) *Kol Sason* 2) *veKol Simchah*, 3) *Kol Chasan*, 4) *veKol Kallah*, 5) *Kol Omrim, Hodu es Hashem* (*Berachos*, 6b). Additionally, there are five *Kinyanim* / acquisitions of Hashem (Mishnah, *Avos*, 6:10). The fifth acquisition listed is the Beis haMikdash. The Beis haMikdash is called "the *Hod* / splendor of the world" (*Berachos*, 58a).

What is the nature of this inner relationship between 'five' and Hod, as we see expressed in so many various verses? 'Five' represents a step beyond the dynamic of duality, of pairs. 'Five' is also a step beyond the world of space and time; there are three dimensions of space, and the fourth dimension is time. With regard to the four cardinal directions of space we could say that the 'fifth' is the single 'point' in the center, which is not located along any vector of the four directions, but is the source point of them all. This point is also one with the exact location of the subject, the 'individual' who is charting the directions.

Five is beyond polarity — alluding to total humility. However, this unitive consciousness paradoxically 'includes' the individual. The highest or most essential level of soul, the *Yechidah* / Unified, is alluded to by the prayer of gratitude, *Modeh Ani*. *Modeh* means *Hoda'ah*, complete submission, humility, self-nullification. Yet there is also an *Ani* / I; the wholeness of Yechidah includes the ego-self within it. The highest level thus includes the lowest.

Lag b'Omer, the 'fifth of the fifth,' is the *Chai* (18th) / life of Iyyar, signifying the inner quality of this special month as well as the revelation of our living 'essence.'

Highest of the High and the Lowest of the Low are Unified

The Gemara mentions that the waving of the Omer pushes aside the "negative winds." "Waving one's offering back and forth counteracts [negativity emanating from] the four corners of the world, and the waving up and down…" (*Sukkah*, 37b. *Menachos*, 62a). Additionally, the Medrash Rabbah (*Chukas*) mentions that our daily counting during the seven weeks of the Omer wards off the negative winds of the world. These teachings are identical with the reasons given for waving the Lulav on Sukkos — to neutralize or redirect any negative energy coming from the four directions.

The four cardinal directions, plus up and down, form a six-sided cube. The *Nekudah* / point in the center of the cube is the seventh direction. In terms of the Sefiros, there are two ways of correlating these points with the directions. This first map is identical to the Sefirah-correlations when we wave the Lulav according to the more known custom

Cardinal Direction	Relative Direction	Week of Omer	Sefirah
South	Right	Week One	Chesed
North	Left	Week Two	Gevurah
East	Front	Week Three	Tiferes
Up	Above	Week Four	Netzach
Down	**Below**	**Week Five**	**Hod**
West	Back	Week Six	Yesod
Center Point	Within	Week Seven	Malchus

The second map follows the progression of directions beginning with the 'four winds' then proceeding to up and down. This is an alternative pairing of Sefirah-combinations and Lulav-waving directions, lesser known than the first version above, but still used by some

Cardinal Direction	Relative Direction	Week of Omer	Sefirah
South	Right	Week One	Chesed
North	Left	Week Two	Gevurah
East	Front	Week Three	Tiferes
West	Back	Week Four	Netzach
Up	**Above**	**Week Five**	**Hod**
Down	Below	Week Six	Yesod
Center Point	Within	Week Seven	Malchus

In this map, the fifth waving, corresponding to Hod, is directed above, rather than below, as in the more widely used version previously mentioned. The fifth day of the fifth week therefore represents the 'above of the above,' the highest of the high. This is Hod as splendor, rather than humility. Together, these two maps reveal to us the fact that the lowliness of total humility elevates us to the highest, most splendorous level of consciousness. The 'lowest of the low' is therefore one with the 'highest of the high.' This is the *Yichud* / Unity of space that we are able to achieve during Sukkos by waving the Lulav.

Rashbi's revelation on *Chai* Iyyar, the fifth day of the fifth week of the Omer, embodies the *Yichud* / Unity of time — the oneness of all past and present exiles along with the future Redemption. Rashbi's mystical teachings, collected in the Zohar, also reveal the fifth level of soul, the *Yechidah* / Unity of consciousness, which includes both the highest spiritual levels as well as the lowest manifestations of ego. Lag b'Omer is the paradigmatic day of *Yichud* / Unity and *Etzem* / Essence.

Other Books by the Author

RECLAIMING THE SELF
The Way of Teshuvah

Teshuvah is one of the great gifts of life. It speaks of a hope for a better today and empowers us to choose a brighter tomorrow. But what exactly is Teshuvah? How does it work? How can we undo our past and how do we deal with guilt? And what is healthy regret without eroding our self-esteem? In this fascinating and empowering book, the path for genuine transformation and a way to include all of our past in the powerful moment of the now, is explored and demonstrated.

THE MYSTERY OF KADDISH
Understanding the Mourner's Kaddish

The Mystery of Kaddish is an in-depth exploration into the Mourner's Prayer. Throughout Jewish history, there have been many rites and rituals associated with loss and mourning, yet none have prevailed quite like the Mourner's Kaddish Prayer, which has become the definitive ritual of mourning. The book explores the source of this prayer and deconstructs the meaning to better understand the grieving process and how the Kaddish prayer supports and uplifts the bereaved through their own personal journey to healing.

UPSHERNISH: The First Haircut
Exploring the Laws, Customs & Meanings of a Boy's First Haircut

What is the meaning of Upsherin, the traditional celebration of a boy's first haircut at the age of three? Why is a boy's hair allowed to grow freely for his first three years? What is the deeper import of hair in all its lengths and varieties? What is the meaning of hair coverings? Includes a guide to conducting an Upsherin ceremony.

A BOND FOR ETERNITY
Understanding the Bris Milah

What is the Bris Milah – the covenant of circumcision? What does it represent, symbolize and signify? This book provides an in depth and sensitive review of this fundamental Mitzvah. In this little masterpiece of wisdom – profound yet accessible —the deeper meaning of this essential rite of passage and its eternal link to the Jewish people, is revealed and explored.

REINCARNATION AND JUDAISM
The Journey of the Soul

A fascinating analysis of the concept of Gilgul / Reincarnation. Dipping into the fountain of ancient wisdom and modern understanding, this book addresses and answers such basic questions as: What is reincarnation? Why does it occur? And how does it affect us personally?

INNER RHYTHMS
The Kabbalah of MUSIC

Exploring the inner dimension of sound and music, and particularly, how music permeates all aspects of life. The topics range from Deveikus/Unity and Yichudim/Unifications, to the more personal issues, such as Simcha/Happiness and Marirus/ sadness.

MEDITATION AND JUDAISM
Exploring the Jewish Meditative Paths

A comprehensive work encompassing the entire spectrum of Jewish thought, from the sages of the Talmud and the early Kabbalists to the modern philosophers and Chassidic masters. This book is both a scholarly, in-depth study of meditative practices, and a practical, easy to follow guide for any person interested in meditating the Jewish way.

TOWARD THE INFINITE

A book focusing exclusively on the Chassidic approach to meditation known as Hisbonenus. Encompassing the entire meditative experience, it takes the reader on a comprehensive and engaging journey through this unique practice. The book explores the various states of consciousness that a person encounters in the course of the meditation, beginning at a level of extreme self-awareness and concluding with a state of total non-awareness.

THIRTY – TWO GATES OF WISDOM
Awakening through Kabbalah

Kabbalah holds the secrets to a path of conscious awareness. In this compact book, 32 key concepts of Kabbalah are explored and their value in opening the gates of perception are demonstrated.

THE PURIM READER
The Holiday of Purim Explored

With a Persian name, a masquerade dress code and a woman as the heroine, Purim is certainly unusual amongst the Jewish holidays. Most people are very familiar with the costumes, Megilah and revelry, but are mystified by their significance. This book offers a glimpse into the hidden world of Purim, uncovering these mysteries and offering a deeper understanding of this unique holiday.

EIGHT LIGHTS
8 Meditations for Chanukah

What is the meaning and message of Chanukah? What is the spiritual significance of the Lights of the Menorah? What are the Lights telling us? What is the deeper dimension of the Dreidel? Rav Pinson, with his trademark deep learning and spiritual sensitivity guides us through eight meditations relating to the Lights of the Menorah, the eight days of Chanukah, and a fascinating exploration of the symbolism and structure of the Dreidel. Includes a detailed how-to guide for lighting the Chanukah Menorah.

THE IYYUN HAGADAH
An Introduction to the Haggadah

In this beautifully written introduction to Passover and the Haggadah, we are guided through the major themes of Passover and the Seder night. This slim text, addresses the important questions, such as: What is the big deal of Chametz? What are we trying to achieve through conducting a Seder? What's with all that stuff on the Seder Plate? And most importantly, how is this all related to freedom?

PASSPORT TO KABBALAH
A Journey of Inner Transformation

Life is a journey full of ups and downs, inside-outs, and unexpected detours. There are times when we think we know exactly where we want to be headed, and other times when we are so lost we don't even know where we are. This slim book provides readers with a passport of sorts to help them through any obstacles along their path of self-refinement, reflection, and self-transformation.

THE FOUR SPECIES
The Symbolism of the Lulav & Esrog

The Four Species have inspired countless commentaries and traditions and intrigued scholars and mystics alike. In this little masterpiece of wisdom both profound and practical - the deep symbolic roots and nature of the Four Species are explored. The Na'anuim, or ritual of the Lulav movement, is meticulously detailed and Kavanos,, are offered for use with the practice. Includes an illustrated guide to the Lulav Movements.

THE BOOK OF LIFE AFTER LIFE

What is a soul? What happens to us after we physically die?

What is consciousness, and can it survive without a physical brain?

Can we remember our past lives?

Do near-death experiences prove immortality?

What is Gan Eden? Resurrection?

Exploring the possibility of surviving death, the near-death experience and a glimpse into what awaits us after this life.

(This book is an updated and expanded version of the book; Jewish Wisdom of the Afterlife)

THE GARDEN OF PARADOX:
The Essence of Non - Dual Kabbalah

This book is a Primer on the Essential Philosophy of Kabbalah presented as a series of 3 conversations, revealing the mysteries of Creator, Creation and Consciousness. With three representational students, embodying respectively, the philosopher, the activist and the mystic, the book, tackles the larger questions of life. Who is G-d? Who am I? Why do I exist? What is my purpose in this life? Written in clear and concise prose, the text, gently guides the reader towards making sense of life's paradoxes and living meaningfully.

BREATHING & QUIETING THE MIND

Achieving a sense of self-mastery and inner freedom demands that we gain a measure of hegemony over our thoughts. We learn to choose out thoughts so that we are not at the mercy of whatever belches up to the mind. Through quieting the mind and conscious breathing we can slow the onrush of anxious, scattered thinking and come to a deeper awareness of the interconnectedness of all of life.

Source texts are included in translation, with how-to-guides for the various practices.

VISUALIZATION AND IMAGERY:
Harnessing the Power of our Mind's Eye

We assume that what we see with our eyes is absolute. Yet, beyond our ability to choose what we see, we have the ability to choose how we see. This directly translates into how we experience life. In a world saturated with visual imagery, our senses are continuously assaulted with Kelipa/empty/fantasy imagery that we would not necessarily choose. These images can negatively affect our relationship with ourselves, with the world around us, and with the Divine. This volume seeks to show us how we can alter that which we observe through harnessing the power of our mind's eye, the inner sanctum of our imagination. We thus create a new way to see and experience the world. This book teaches us how to utilize visualization and imagery as a way to develop our spiritual sensitivity and higher intuition, and ultimately achieve Deveikus/Unity with Hashem.

THE POWER OF CHOICE:
A Practical Guide to Conscious Living

It is the essential premise of this book that we hold the key to unlock many of the gates that seem closed to us and keep us from living our fullest life. That key we all hold is the power to choose. The Power of Choice is the primary tool that we have at our disposal to impact the world and effect change within our own lives. We often give up this power to outside forces such as the market, media, politicians or peer pressure; or to internal forces that often function beyond our conscious control such as ego, anger, lust, greed or jealousy. Making conscious, compassionate and creative decisions is the cornerstone of living a mature and meaningful life.

MYSTIC TALES FROM THE EMEK HAMELECH

Mystic Tales of the Emek HaMelech, is a wondrous and inspiring collection of stories culled from the Emek HaMelech. Emek HaMelech, from which these stories have been taken, (as well as its author) is a bit of a mystery. But like all good mysteries, it is one worth investigating. In this spirit the present volume is being offered to the general public in the merit and memory of its saintly author, as well as in the hopes of introducing a vital voice of deeper Torah teaching and tradition to a contemporary English speaking audience

INNER WORLDS OF JEWISH PRAYER
A Guide to Develop and Deepen the Prayer Experience

While much attention has been paid to the poetry, history, theology and contextual meaning of the prayers, the intention of this work is to provide a guide to finding meaning and effecting transformation through the prayer experience itself.

Explore: *What happens when we pray? *How do we enter the mind-state of prayer? *Learning to incorporate the body into the prayers. *Discover techniques to enhance and deepen prayer and make it a transformative experience.

This empowering and inspiring text, demonstrates how through proper mindset, preparation and dedication, the experience of prayer can be deeply transformative and ultimately, life-altering.

WRAPPED IN MAJESTY
Tefillin - Exploring the Mystery

Tefillin, the black boxes and leather straps that are worn during prayer, are curiously powerful and mysterious. Within the inky black boxes lie untold secrets. In this profound, passionate and thought-provoking text, the multi-dimensional perspectives of Tefillin are explored and revealed. Magically weaving together all levels of Torah including the Peshat (literal observation), to Remez (allegorical), to Derush, (homiletic), to Sod (hidden) into one beautiful tapestry. Inspirational and instructive, Wrapped in Majesty: Tefillin, will make putting on the Tefillin more meaningful and inspiring.

Now Available!

A 12 Part Series on the Months of the Year.

The rest of this series is being published book by book.

THE SPIRAL OF TIME:
Unraveling the Yearly Cycle

Many centuries ago, the Sages of Israel were the foremost authority in the fields of both astronomical calculation and astrological wisdom, including the deeper interpretations of the cycles and seasons. Over time, this wisdom became hidden within the esoteric teachings of the Torah, and as a result was known only to students and scholars of the deepest depths of the tradition. More recently, the great teachers, from R.Yitzchak Luria (the Arizal) to the Baal Shem Tov, taught that as the world approaches the Era of Redemption, it is a Mitzvah / spiritual obligation to broadly reveal this wisdom.

"The Spiral of Time" is volume 1 is a series of 12 books, and serves as an introductory book to the basic concepts and nature of the Hebrew calendar and explores the special day of Rosh Chodesh.

THE MONTH OF SHEVAT: ELEVATING EATING
& The Holiday of Tu b'Shevat

Each month of the year radiates with a distinct quality and provides unique opportunities for personal growth and illumination. Shevat falls decidedly in the winter season, yet it also signals the first stirrings of spring and new life. The midpoint of the month, Tu b'Shevat, is a day we celebrate as the "New Year of the Trees," which represents the awakening of the sap that has lain dormant all winter. The mental, emotional, and spiritual objective of this month is to create healthy relationships with our physical appetites — and most specifically with food. Explore the corresponding symbols, themes, Divine Names, body parts, Torah portions and mystical teachings as brought down in Kabbalah and Chassidus that illuminate this unique month.

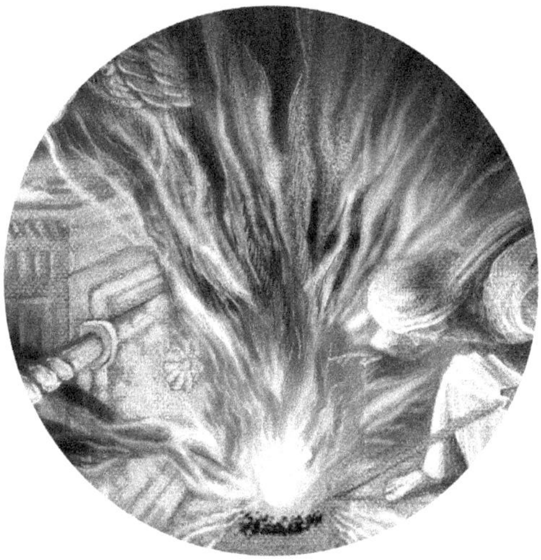